THE WORLD OF DOC HOLLIDAY

ISBN 0-9643343-0-5
ISBN 0-9643343-1-3 (Hard Bound)
First edition, September 1994

BOOK ONE

————◆·◆————

The Illustrated Life And Times of
Doc Holliday

*"The essential
American soul is
hard, isolate, stoic
and a killer."*
—D.H. LAWRENCE

*For ★ ♥ Michele
Stay clean of the trees!*
12/19/94

BY BOB BOZE BELL

A LIMITED EDITION

JOHN HENRY HOLLIDAY AND HIS MOTHER, ALICE JANE McKEY HOLLIDAY
This never-before-published ambrotype, circa 1852, shows Baby-Doc eying the world from his mother's lap. Even as a tyke, John Henry Holliday evidences a gaze which will dismay and unnerve many a card sharp across a gaming room table in later years.

BRIGHT-EYED BOY

When the future lay bright with promise—a twenty-year-old John H. Holliday as he looks when attending the Pennsylvania College of Dental Surgery. Before the cough, before the whiskey—when he still believes in a "normal life." (BY BBB, FROM A PHOTOGRAPH)

DOC IN PRESCOTT, 1879

DRUNK AS A SKUNK
"*He was not a drunkard. He always had a bottle of whiskey but never drank habitually. When he needed a drink, he would take only a small one.*"
—*Kate* (BBB)

DOC'S FLASK?
A recently discovered whiskey flask inscribed, "To Doctor J. H. Holiday (sic) from his friend E.Z.C. Judson (Ned Buntline)" (see closeup at right). (COURTESY JAN HARRISON)

"This is Funny"
—Doc Holliday

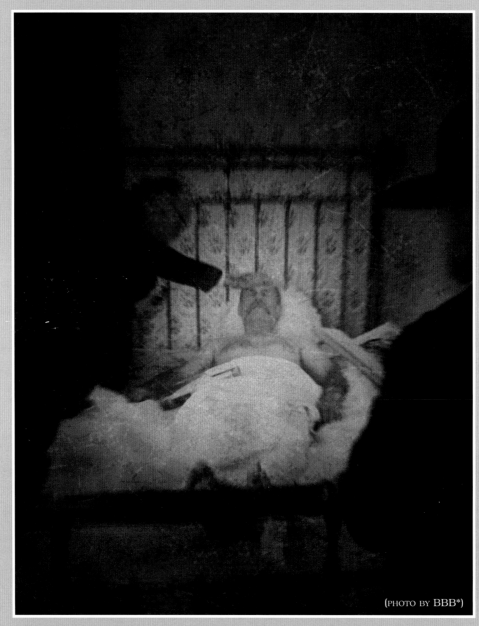

(PHOTO BY BBB*)

THE FINAL JOKE
Overlooking Glenwood Springs, Colorado is a cemetery with a monument to the memory of the West's most famous dentist. He's not there. (PHOTOS BY BBB)

PART ONE

"A Doc is Delivered"

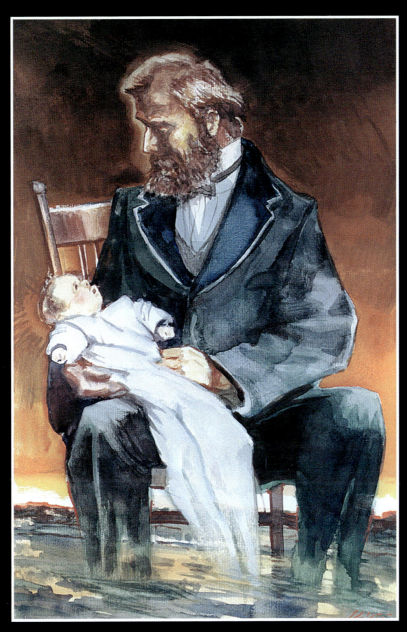

On August 14, 1851 Major Henry B. Holliday becomes the father of his only son. Tragically, he outlives his son but not the legend.

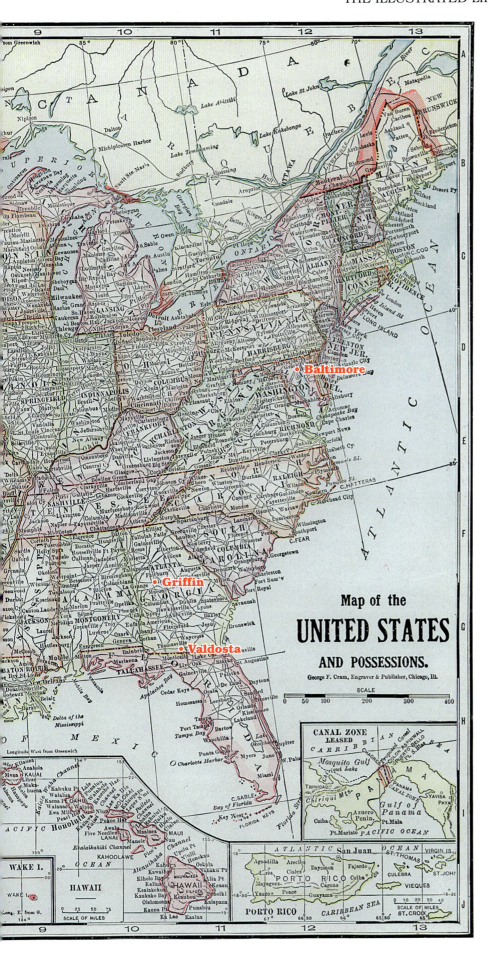

DOC'S WEST

It is tempting to speculate that if it had not been for tuberculosis, the trail of John Henry Holliday would have very likely remained along the East Coast. Unlike other pioneer families (like the Earps) who headed for the western horizon as a brood, the Hollidays stayed pretty close to home. It was left for Doc to banish himself out into the unknown and onto death's trail. That trail led him through a relatively narrow vale—consider all the places he didn't go—California, the Northwest, Mexico, to name but a few.

JOHN HENRY AS A STUDENT
(BY BBB, FROM A PHOTOGRAPH)

August 14, 1851
John Henry Holliday is born in Spalding County, Georgia.

March 21, 1852
John Henry Holliday is baptized at First Presbyterian Church in Griffin, Georgia.

May 20, 1861
North Carolina votes to secede from the Union.

September, 1861
Civil War—Henry B. Holliday, Doc's father, serves in the Quartermaster Corps of the 27th Regiment of Georgia at Camp Pickens, Manassas, Virginia— under Beauregard.

December 25, 1861
Henry B. Holliday is promoted to Major.

July 27, 1862
Major Holliday tenders his resignation due to ill health (chronic diarrhea).

Major Holliday Heads for the Rear (WOODCUT BY BBB)

February 9, 1864
Major Holliday purchases 2,450 acres near Bemiss in Lowndes County, Georgia for $31,500.

August 30, 1864
Doc's uncle, Robert Kennedy Holliday, sends his wife and two daughters to seek refuge at his brother Henry's residence. One of the girls—Mattie—forms a close friendship with young John.

Doc's home in Valdosta, Georgia, as it appears in the early 1970s. (ILLUSTRATED BY BRAD S. RUMINER, FROM A PHOTOGRAPH)

During the Civil War, as troops sweep back and forth across Georgia, Union troops often camp in the yards of southern homes (above). *For this reason, Major Holliday has his sister's family join his.* (TIMOTHY SULLIVAN PHOTO)

DOC HOLLIDAY'S FAMILY HISTORY

BATTLE OF MONTERREY, 1847

1660

Thomas Holliday and Mary Hardy Hinton come over from England to settle in Jamestown, Virginia. These are the first ancestors of Doc on record. Exact relationship not indicated.

June 4, 1818

Robert Alexander Holliday and Rebecca Burroughs (Doc's grandparents) marry in South Carolina.

March 11, 1819

Henry Burroughs Holliday (Doc's father) is born in Laurens County, South Carolina.

April 21, 1829

Alice Jane McKey (Doc's mother) is born in South Carolina.

May 12, 1838–June 20, 1838

Holding the rank of 2nd Lieutenant in Capt. John D. Stills Company of 1st Georgia Volunteers, Doc's father serves in the Cherokee Indian War.

June 11, 1846-June 30, 1847

The Mexican War—As 2nd Lieutenant, Henry B. Holliday serves in "The Fannin Avengers" under Harrison J. Sargent. This company, in turn, becomes part of a regiment commanded by Col. Henry R. Jackson of Savannah, Georgia. Holliday sees service on the upper line to Monterrey, Mexico under General Zachary Taylor and in Vera Cruz and Jalapa under General Winfield Scott. He is discharged at Jalapa, Mexico.

1847

Though still a bachelor, when Henry B. Holliday returns to Georgia, he brings with him a small ten-year-old orphaned Mexican boy—Francisco Hidalgo. He raises the boy himself.

January 8, 1849

Henry B. Holliday (29 years old) marries Alice Jane McKey (19 years old).

December 3, 1849

Doc's sister, Martha Elanora Holliday, is born.

June 12, 1850

Little Martha, age 6 months, 9 days, dies.

December, 1850

Spalding County, Georgia is created. Henry B. Holliday becomes the first clerk of the Superior Court of Spalding County.

May 24, 1865

With the war over, Robert Holliday takes his family back to their own home.

Note

Young John Holliday completes grade school at the Valdosta Institute—a private school. Exact years of attendance are unknown. The classics are stressed. Greek, Latin and French are studied as a matter of course.

September 16, 1866

After years of failing health, Doc's mother dies. Young John takes the death very hard. The general feeling is that Mrs. Henry B. Holliday succumbs to tuberculosis, which is commonplace among the malnourished and hard-pressed people of the South during the war. Tragically, young John probably contracted the disease from his own mother. She is 37, one year older than Doc will be when death finally takes him.

December 18, 1866

The widowed Major Holliday (47-years-old) marries 23-year-old Rachel Martin. This ready marriage sparks discord between Doc and his father. Betrayal is a sin John will forever despise.

1866-1872

In February 1872, Doc's uncles, Thomas S. and William H. McKey, purchase land on the Withlacoochee River. With his friends, young John Holliday clears out an area to serve as their own private swimming hole. Now with his uncle Thomas, Holliday takes a buggy ride to check out the favored site. Upon arrival John is outraged by the spectacle of free Negroes frolicking in the water. Cautioned by his uncle to "fire over their heads!" John Henry Holliday pulls a Colt's 1851 Navy revolver and lets loose, scattering the interlopers to the four winds. No one is hit, but word of mouth

Valdosta Institute, where Doc attends grammar school and is educated in the classics. (SARAH CRANFORD BRADFORD)

"In Valdosta and the vicinity, Doc is remembered as a clever youngster with excellent manners bred in the bone of the small fry belonging to his kind and time."
—JOHN MYERS MYERS

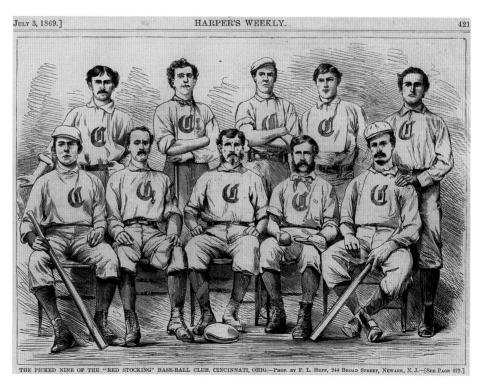

JULY 3, 1869.]   HARPER'S WEEKLY.   421

THE PICKED NINE OF THE "RED STOCKING" BASE-BALL CLUB, CINCINNATI, OHIO.—PHOT. BY F. L. HUFF, 244 BROAD STREET, NEWARK, N. J.—[SEE PAGE 422.]

Harry Wright establishes the first professional baseball team, the Cincinnati "Red Stockings," in 1869. The players earn $1,400 per season.

"Papa said, 'Shoot over their heads!'"
—MRS. CLYDE MCKEY WHITE

This Georgia swimming hole, photographed by Timothy Sullivan during the Civil War, illustrates the type of pond where young Holliday allegedly shot at the freed Negroes. It must be pointed out that there is no verification for this "family story." In fact, the relative who told the story had a similar incident, which may have been extrapolated and attributed to John. (TIMOTHY SULLIVAN PHOTO)

blows the incident out of proportion to become a "minor massacre" of sorts. An aura of danger begins to be associated with Major Holliday's slight lad. (A photo of this gun, which was in the Holliday family for over 100 years, is shown on page 78.) About the same time, a group of angry young Southerners plot to blow up the county courthouse in Valdosta, which headquarters the Freeman's Bureau. Word leaks, the plan is aborted and several ringleaders are forced to leave the area. Rumors have Doc to be one of the schemers.

1872

John Henry Holliday graduates from the Pennsylvania College of Dental Surgery. (Doc's first Cousin, Robert A. Holliday, founded the first school of dentistry in Georgia.)

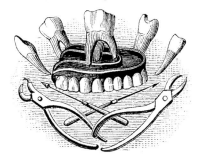

Late 1872

Holliday shares an office with Dr. Arthur C. Ford on the corner of Alabama and Whitehall streets in Atlanta. But because of ill health, Holliday returns to his boyhood hometown of Griffin, Georgia, where he briefly practices dentistry. Bouts of coughing, however, continue until Doc's physician finally renders the dreaded diagnosis—tuberculosis. Doc is advised to go West for the climate. Alternately melancholy and volatile, Doc Holliday heads for Texas.

KATE

Doc's woman is shrouded in a veil almost as thick as his, just out of reach, lying somewhere between the mists of legend and the fog of fiction. However, from various sources a partial sketch of the woman Doc both loved and hated can be constructed.

She was born Mary Katherine Haroney on November 7, 1850. Kate, as she eventually became known, was the oldest of seven children of Doctor Michael and Katherine Baldizar Haroney, who lived in the Pest section of Budapest, Hungary.

Kate's father, Doc Michael, moved his family to the United States and purchased a lot in Davenport, Iowa, in May 1863. It appears that both Kate's parents died in the spring of 1865 (from exactly what, we don't know). After being shipped from one guardian to another, she ran away on a steamboat for points south. (It is tempting to conjecture that since many prostitutes are the victims of sexual abuse, perhaps Kate suffered such mistreatment.)

KATE IN DODGE, 1875 (BBB)

The next place Kate shows up is Wichita in 1874, where a "Kate Elder" pays fines while working in a "sporting house" run by James and Bessie Earp. In 1875, one "Kate Elder" works at Tom Sherman's dance hall in Dodge City. Though Kate later claimed she married Doc at Valdosta, Georgia on May 25, 1876, no record of that union has ever surfaced. In fact, Doc is listed as "single" in all census reports listing him throughout his life.

MARY KATHERINE HARONEY
This is the earliest known photo of Big Nose Kate (seated) and her sister. Location unknown. (SHARLOT HALL MUSEUM LIBRARY/ARCHIVES, PRESCOTT, ARIZONA)

"And Death is on him Dwelling."
—*"Barbara Allen"*
(Old Folk Song)

By 1872 the glory days of river travel are over. The Civil War has so devastated the South, that while gambling and drinking still occupies the travelers' time, the majestic opulence celebrated by Mark Twain is already history.

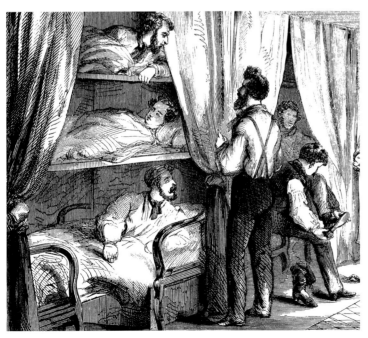

As Doc rides west, by train, he has to sleep in one of three rows of berth. As one wag puts it, "It was like undressing under a sofa."

Doc's Journey West

After the inevitable denial, the terminal prognosis of his disease must have sunk in. Tradition says his doctor gave the 21-year-old John Henry Holliday six months to live. We don't know. There is no record of it. However, he banished himself to the frontier where he intended to meet Death head on and wrote many letters to his cousin Mattie. Perhaps if we could ever read them we would begin to fathom what he was going through. Whatever he was thinking, one thing's for certain: the farther west he went, the more he became a man who was going out of his way to die.

November 12, 1872

The first deeds of lands, left to John by his mother, are sold off to help support him until he can develop a dental practice.

With this money Holliday leaves home and begins his journey west. He takes the train, riding all night across Georgia on Kimball's sleeping cars. The quarters were so cramped and the three rows of berth so close together that Robert Louis Stevenson once commented that going to bed in one was rather like undressing under a sofa.

After an all-night ride, Doc arrives in Chattanooga, Tennessee. From there it is 310 miles and 29 hours to Memphis! (The trains could actually do sixty if the throttle puller let them, but local laws and public opinion held them down to 20 or 30 miles an hour.)

At Memphis, Doc catches the steamer Natchez, and two-and-a-half days later he arrives in New Orleans. (The train saloon featured "Brandy Smashes," "Stone Fences" and "Earthquakes." "Gentleman's games" are another diversion.)

From New Orleans, Doc boards another train for a ninety-mile ride across the peninsula to catch the

Morgan Line iron steamer to Galveston. The fare is $18! But as some wag once said, "Distance is no measure of worth when there's only one way to go."

From Galveston, another wood-burning, bone-crunching train of the Houston and Texas Central delivers the son of Major Holliday into Dallas, Texas.

DOC IN DALLAS

1873

The second deed Major Holliday sells, for his son, is dated March 25, 1873.

In Dallas, Doc meets Dr. John A. Seegar, a former Georgian and fellow dentist with an already established practice. Together they become partners and share an office between Market and Austin streets on Elm (the same Elm Street J.F.K. would be assassinated on 90 years later).

At first Doc practices dentistry in a dedicated way. Unbeknownst to Holliday, his illness has, for some unknown reason, granted him a reprieve. But with every cough, Doc believes his own expiration increasingly imminent. Two avenues, however, offer relief from physical pain and morbid preoccupation. Whiskey wraps both body and soul in sweet, warm oblivion. Gambling is an exercise that focuses the mind on matters at hand. Julian Bogel's saloon soon sees John Henry Holliday transformed into 'Doc' Holliday. To protect himself against physically stronger men, Doc practices with both knife and gun as life insurance. "God may have made all men but, Col. Colt made them equal." Since death is his destiny, Doc makes it his theme. Gradually he becomes a menacing parody of himself. The best defense is a strong offense, so Holliday assumes the persona of one whisky-soaked, bullet-spitting Son o' Thunder whose only saving grace is that he will soon be dead.

For two years the volcano lies

Bat Masterson, circa 1876, in Dodge City, Kansas. Bat doesn't like Doc, and his writings will greatly influence history's image of Holliday. (CRAIG FOUTS PHOTO COLLECTION)

dormant, building up the pressures needed for eruption. This comes on New Year's Day, 1875.

January 1, 1875

"Dr. Holliday and Mr. Austin, a saloon-keeper, relieved the monotony of the noise of fire crackers by taking a couple of shots at each other yesterday afternoon. The cheerful note of the peaceful six-shooter is heard once more among us. Both shooters were arrested." *Dallas Herald*-Jan. 2, 1875.

Apparently Doc made quick egress from Dallas, for on Jan. 12, 1875 he is indicted by the Grand Jury in Fort Griffin, for "gaming in a saloon," along with Hurricane Bill, Liz, Etta, Kate, et al, and charged with keeping a "disorderly house." This is the first published linkage between Doc and Kate.

April 28, 1876

The cornerstone of the Territorial Prison is laid in Yuma. The first prisoners are received here in June.

A VAGUE WANDERING

1875–1877

The movements of Doc Holliday from 1875 to late 1877 are difficult to detail with any precision. Speculation is, he sojourned for some considerable time in Denver under the name Tom McKey. Could be, there were plenty of McKee's or McKay's or McKey's around. In later years, Holliday claims to have dealt faro for Charley Foster at Babbitt's House, 357 Blakes Street. Bat Masterson, in his 1907 *Human*

Life article, says Doc killed a soldier at Jacksboro, Texas before moving up to Denver. No confirmation for this statement has been found. Masterson also claims Doc carved up the face of Bud Ryan with a knife while in Denver. Again, no validation surfaces.

By late 1877, according to Wyatt Earp, Doc and Kate are back in Fort Griffin. Always the snowbird, Wyatt is south for the winter, following the gaming circuit and hoping to track some desperadoes with a price on their head. Years later Kate remembered that Doc and Wyatt met at Fort Griffin although she mis-dated the year as 1876.

September 29, 1877

The first Southern Pacific engine on a regular run enters Arizona through Yuma at eleven p.m. However, the connection with New Mexico and points eastward is still unfinished and through service is several years away.

January to May 1878

Wyatt follows the gambling circuit to Fort Worth. Years later, Wyatt will tell the San Francisco *Examiner* what happened to his newly found friends back in Fort Griffin. Let's let Wyatt tell the story:

"Doc Holliday was spending the evening in a poker game, which was his custom whenever faro bank did not present superior claims on his attention. On his right sat Ed Bailey, who needs no description because he is soon to drop out of this narrative. The trouble began, as it was related to me afterward, by Ed Bailey monkeying with the deadwood, or what people who live in cities call discards. Doc Holliday admonished him once or twice to 'play poker'—which is your seasoned gambler's method of cautioning a friend to stop cheating—but the misguided Bailey persisted in his furtive attentions to the deadwood.

Cow-Boy Clothes Horse?

The period we call the Old West was, in actuality, Victorian in style. It's hard to tell the cow-boys from the dudes. The above illustration is from the English publication *Punch*, 1881, showing three well-dressed gents strutting their stuff. Below, we see three well-dressed cow-boys from Tombstone, 1881. About the only differences between the two groups are the boots and sombreros. In fact, the era was so formal that it was not uncommon for ranchers to work cattle wearing ties.

(Arizona Historical Society)

Finally, having detected him again, Holliday pulled down a pot without showing his hand, which he had a perfect right to do. Thereupon Bailey started to throw his gun around on Holliday, as might have been expected. But before he could pull the trigger, Doc Holliday had jerked a knife out of his breast-pocket and with one sideways sweep had caught Bailey just below the brisket.

Well, that broke up the game, and pretty soon Doc Holliday was sitting cheerfully in the front room of the hotel, guarded while the gamblers clamored for his blood. You see, he had not lived in Fort Griffin very long, while Ed Bailey was well liked. It wasn't long before Big Nose Kate, who had a room downtown, heard about the trouble and went up to take a look at her Doc through a back window. What she saw and heard led her to think that his life wasn't worth ten minutes purchase, and I don't believe it was. There was a shed at the back of the lot, and a horse was stabled in it. She was a kindhearted girl was Kate, for she went to the trouble of leading the horse into the alley and tethering it there before she set fire to the shed. She also got a six-shooter from a friend down the street, which, with the one she always carried, made two.

It all happened just as she had planned it. The shed blazed up and she hammered at the door, yelling, "Fire!" Everybody rushed out, except the marshal and the constables and their prisoner. Kate walked in as bold as a lion, threw one of her six-shooters on the marshal and handed the other to Doc Holliday.

"Come on, Doc," she said with a laugh.

He didn't need any second invitation and the two of them backed out of the hotel, keeping the officers covered. All that night they hid in the willows down by the creek, and early next morning a friend of Kate's brought them two horses and some of Doc

Holliday's clothes from his room. Kate dressed up in a pair of pants, a pair of boots, a shirt and a hat, and the pair of them got away safely and rode the four hundred miles to Dodge City, where they were installed in great style when I got back home."

June 8, 1878

The *Dodge City Times* runs an ad:

"Dentistry. J.H. Holliday, Dentist, very respectfully offers his professional services to the citizens of Dodge City and surrounding country for the summer. Office at room No. 24, Dodge House. Where satisfaction is not given money will be refunded."

(ILLUSTRATION BY BRAD RUMINER)

THE DODGE HOUSE
When Doc arrives in Dodge, this is where he stays. The town is awash with drovers fresh off the long drives from Texas. While Doc perfunctorily offers his services as a dentist, the gaming rooms provide him with his real income.

DODGE CITY POLICEMEN MASTERSON & EARP, 1876
Bat Masterson (standing) rests his right hand on his six-shooter. The weapon is worn butt forward, cavalry style, to be pulled with a twist draw. Seated is a stern 28-year-old Wyatt Earp. Both are wearing what appear to be soft leather gunbelts. The scroll-shaped object on Wyatt's chest is the style of badge favored by Dodge City police in the 1870s.

"His whole heart and soul were wrapped up in Wyatt Earp..."
—BAT MASTERSON,
DESCRIBING DOC HOLLIDAY

July 26, 1878

Eddie Foy is performing at the Comique. In the audience are Bat Masterson and Doc Holliday. Wyatt Earp is on duty as assistant town marshal, but he posts himself in front of the theater to hear Foy's act.

In his autobiography, *Clowning Through Life*, Foy recalled that night:

"It had come to be one of my jobs to call the figures for the old-time square dances which were the favorites at Dodge—'All balance left! Swing the right hand lady! Alamon right!'—whatever that may mean; I don't know to this day—and at intervals of twenty minutes or so, 'Balance all to the bar!'—a broad suggestion to everybody to buy a drink. We were going merrily on with the dance when suddenly, Bang! Bang! Bang! came a roar of eight or ten big pistols from the outer darkness, the crash of glass from our windows and shrieks from the women.

Everybody dropped to the floor at once, according to custom. Bat Masterson was just in the act of dealing in a game of Spanish monte with Doc Holliday, and I was impressed by the instantaneous manner in which they flattened out like pancakes on the floor. I had thought I was pretty agile myself, but those fellows had me beaten by seconds at that trick."

1878

It was sometime during this period that the defining moment between Doc Holliday and Wyatt Earp happened. Wyatt remembered that, "It wasn't long after I returned to Dodge City that his [Holliday's] quickness saved my life. He saw a man draw on me behind my back. 'Look out, Wyatt!' he shouted, but while the words were coming out of his mouth he had jerked his pistol out of his pocket and shot the other fellow before the latter could fire."

"On such incidents as that are built the friendships of the frontier."

Stuart Lake's book has Wyatt being held at bay by a hoard of woolly Texans. Critical historians have doubted the incident occurred because Lake's hyperbolic account wasn't validated by the papers. However, an item in the August 20, 1878, *Globe* may be a garbled account of the incident.

"It appears that one of the cowboys, becoming intoxicated and quarrelsome, undertook to take possession of the bar in the Comique. To this the barkeeper objected and a row ensued. Several cattle men then engaged in the brawl and in the excitement some of them were bruised on the head with six-shooters. Several shots were accidentally fired which created general confusion among the crowd of persons present. We are glad to chronicle the fact that none were seriously hurt and nobody shot."

Spring, 1879

A call goes to Dodge City for guns to fight in the Royal Gorge War in Colorado. A silver strike at Leadville has inspired a battle between the Santa Fe line and the Denver & Rio Grande. Both companies are racing to build the first line into Leadville. Trouble is the only feasible route to the silver camp is forged through Royal Gorge. While legal contestation unfolds, the Santa Fe puts a call into Dodge City for men to hold the gorge against the Denver & Rio Grande.

March 25, 1879

—The *Ford County Globe:*

"Last Thursday evening, Sheriff Masterson received a telegram from officers of the Atchison, Topeka and Santa Fe road at Carson City, asking if he could bring a posse of men to assist in defending the workmen on that

THE DOCTOR SAVES A LIFE

road from the attacks of the Denver and Rio Grande men, who were again endeavoring to capture the long-contested pass through the canyon. Masterson and Deputy Duffey immediately opened a recruiting office, and before the train arrived Friday morning had enrolled a company of thirty-three men. They all boarded the morning train, armed to the teeth, Sheriff Masterson in command, and started for the scene of hostilities."

Since it was the Santa Fe that gave Dodge its place in the sun, the town holds a mutual bias in the matter. Among the gunmen who take up with Masterson are John Joshua Webb, Ben Thompson and Doc Holliday.

Eddie Foy says, "The Santa Fe, being 'our own road,' had Dodge's

FORTIFICATIONS IN THE ROYAL GORGE
(DENVER PUBLIC LIBRARY, WESTERN HISTORY DEPT.)

sympathy in the quarrel and, besides there was promise of good pay for the fighters. Doc Holliday suggested that I join them.

"But listen, Mr. Holliday," said I, "I'm no fighter. I wouldn't be any help to the gang. I couldn't hit a man if I shot at him."

"Oh, that's all right," he replied, easily. "The Santy Fee won't know the difference. You kin use a shotgun if you want to. Dodge wants to make a good showin' in this business. You'll help swell the crowd, and you'll get your pay, anyhow."

But I declined to join the

"I am a friend of Doc Holliday because when I was city marshal, of Dodge City, Kansas, he came to my rescue and saved my life when I was surrounded by desperadoes."
—WYATT EARP

expedition, much to Doc's disappointment. Twenty men went from Dodge, headed by Ben Thompson, a Texas man and a dangerous character who made his home for a while among us. From time to time, reports of the progress of the war came back to us from the front. It was even rumored along Main Street that our brave lads had held the round-house at Pueblo for several hours against a large detachment of United States soldiers. Finally, the two roads compromised the matter, greatly to the disgust of certain citizens of Dodge who had been hoping that the home boys would be permitted to wipe the D. & R.G. off the map."

1879

It's not known if Doc returned to Dodge City after his service for the Santa Fe. Bat Masterson claims Holliday "went from Dodge to Trinidad, Colorado, where within a week from the time he landed, he shot and seriously wounded a young sport by the name of Kid Colton, over a very trivial matter. He was again forced to hunt the tall timber and managed to make his escape to Las Vegas, New Mexico, which was then something of a boom town, on account of the Santa Fe Railroad having just reached there." (1907 *Human Life* article)

Again, no newspaper confirmation of the Trinidad shooting is found. Whatever the case, by summer, Doc Holliday is running a saloon in Las Vegas, New Mexico.

According to Miguel Otero, Doc shot and wounded one Charley White in June of 1880. Since Holliday was by that time at Prescott, if the incident occurred, it would be June, 1879.

March, 1879

Doc Holliday is fined $25 during the March term of court for keeping an illegal gaming table in East Las Vegas, New Mexico.

The "Hanging Windmill," on the Las Vegas Plaza, served vigilantes as a handy scaffold until residences complained of blood in the water supply. It was demolished one night, in 1880, by irate citizens. (MUSEUM OF NEW MEXICO, NEGATIVE 14386.)

THE DODGE CITY GANG INVADES LAS VEGAS

Hoodoo Brown ruled East Las Vegas during its formative period. A newspaper described his tenure thusly:

"[Hoodoo Brown] has been in the western wilds for many years, and for a long time was one of the worst class of low gamblers. A recital of the many terrible affairs with which he has been connected in this country would make a whole book of horribles. When he came here, there was a great bustle and excitement with building houses and railroads, and the rughs and gamblers being the only idle ones, had things pretty much their own way, and elected him justice of the peace and coroner. He conducted his business in a fearless manner, and rather won the admiration of the citizens, although they always mistrusted him. "The novel way in which he always opened court contains a little grim humor and illustrates how law reigned here but a few months ago. He would seat himself and say, "Myself and my partner will now open court," pointing to a large, double-barreled Winchester lying against the desk at his side."

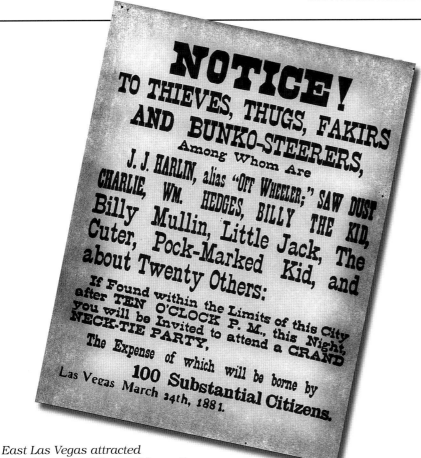

East Las Vegas attracted a motley crew of "bagged-legged" characters, who were finally and formally asked to leave in March of 1882. (This widely reproduced poster is often back-dated to 1881 so the Billy the Kid listed in the text fits the lifespan of the most famous Billy the Kid, Billy Bonney, who died in July 1881.)

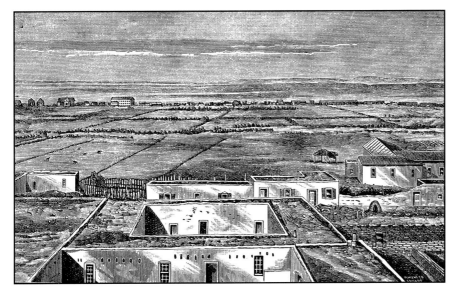

WEST VERSES EAST LAS VEGAS

When the Santa Fe Railroad bypasses Las Vegas, a new town springs up along the tracks several miles to the east. (Seen in the distance.) Thus—East Las Vegas. It is there Doc Holliday and the rest of the Dodge City Gang congregate.

DOC WOULD HAVE LOVED THIS —A GIN FIZZ ON THE SANTA FE TRAIL! (CONTEMPORARY WOODCUT, CIRCA 1870'S)

Shortly after this, Doc opens his last dental office but quickly abandons the practice when he opens his own saloon on Centre Street in July.

July 19, 1879

Mike Gordon goes on a tear at Holliday's saloon. Involved with a saloon girl who works at Doc's place, Gordon tries to get her to quit her job. When she refuses, Mike is inclined to shoot up the liquor emporium. From the street, Gordon puts two shots into the building. Coolly, Doc steps outside, pulls his shooter and fells Gordon with one shot. Mike Gordon dies the next day.

July 26, 1879

The Santa Fe Railroad has bypassed Las Vegas, New Mexico by several miles to the east and now a new town has sprung up along the tracks. This new municipality is mostly saloons and is ruled by Hoodoo Brown, real name Hyman G. Neil, and his so-called Dodge City Gang. Doc Holliday is intimate with all of these scallywags and fits right in. Meanwhile, another alumni from the Dodge City Gang is about to join him.

October, 1879

Wyatt Earp, having resigned his position in Dodge City, is on his way to Arizona. Inspired by the silver strike in a desolate spot in Southeastern Arizona Territory called, ominously enough, Tombstone. When Wyatt and

Mattie come through Las Vegas, brother James, with wife and kids, accompanies them. Doc and Kate decide to hitch their hopes on the same dark star as the Earps and join the caravan. Their first destination is Prescott to hook up with Virgil and Allie Earp. While there, Doc delights in the town. A lucky streak at the gaming tables imbues the quaint town with an unexpected luster.

November, 1879

The Earps push on. Doc and his woman stay on in Prescott to ride out their roll of luck.

1880

At an Industrial Exhibition in Paris, France the Perreaux steam velocipede (a motorized tri-cycle) is showcased—top speed is 15 to 18 miles an hour.

June 2, 1880

JOHN J. GOSPER

When the Earps leave Prescott in November of 1879, Doc and Kate stay in the mile-high city. Doc Holliday shows up on the Prescott, A.T. census. He is rooming on Montezuma Street with two men, Richard E. Elliott, 45 (a good friend of Virgil Earp); and John J. Gosper, 39, the acting governor of Arizona. (Gosper is the secretary of state, but the official governor, John C. Fremont, is rarely in the territory and the duties fall to Doc's roommate.) It's unclear where Kate is during this time.

Stuart Lake will later claim in his book "Frontier Marshal" that Doc hit a winning streak playing

Montezuma Street, Prescott, A.T., 1874 (SHARLOT HALL MUSEUM LIBRARY/ARCHIVES, PRESCOTT, ARIZONA.)

North Montezuma Street, Prescott, A.T., 1881. It is perhaps in this very boarding house, at left, that Doc Holliday roomed with the acting governor of Arizona, John J. Gosper. This nugget of Arizona history has dismayed many Holliday researchers, who are deeply disappointed that Doc would have sunk so low as to have roomed with a politician. (SHARLOT HALL MUSEUM LIBRARY/ARCHIVES, PRESCOTT, ARIZONA.)

DOC DEALS FARO AS WYATT EARP LOOKS ON

It's Cee-gar City as Doc Holliday deals faro to a wary trio of gamblers who are "Bucking the Tiger." This could be Prescott, or Tombstone, or Tucson, or Las Vegas, or Dodge, or Leadville, or Pueblo or any of the stops in between. This is a scene that repeats itself countless times, with Holliday on either side of the table—Doc doesn't care, he deals faro and plays it, around the clock. Breathing the smoky, stale air night after night must do nothing to help his condition. (BY BBB)

**5TH GOVERNOR
JOHN C. FREMONT**

faro on Whiskey Row and ran up a $10,000 poke, but one Earp historian thinks the figure is wildly inflated, stating, "Doc Holliday never saw that much money in his life." Surprisingly, for those who imagine Doc and Wyatt joined at the hip, Holliday doesn't get to Tombstone until about ten months after the Earps arrive.

"In a short time those who wished to consult professionally with the doctor, had to do so over a card table in some nearby gambling establishment, or not at all."
—BAT MASTERSON

TURBULENT TOMBSTONE

May, 1879

The population of the village of Tombstone is 250. The Tombstone Townsite Company is formed.

1879 (Day and month unknown)

Johnny Ringo shoots Louis Hancock in the jaw during a drunken quarrel in a Safford, Arizona saloon. (Although he will amass quite a reputation as a gunman, this is the only shooting Ringo is ever tied to in Arizona.)

November and December, 1879

The "Pinafore on Wheels" theatrical group headed by Pauline Markham (see page 40) tours Arizona, hitting Prescott and Tombstone. Among the cast members is an 18-year-old dark-haired Jewish beauty from San Francisco named Josephine Sarah Marcus. As the troupe makes its approach to Prescott, a group of mounted men ride out to escort the ladies in. One of them is Johnny Behan, and Miss Marcus is immediately struck with his handsome ways and debonair style.

May 4, 1880

The first of many fires sweeps the village of Tombstone. The Tucson *Citizen* reports, "The fire occurred about 1 o'clock in Gray & McLane's Stables which adjoined P.W. Smith's Store. It originated in the southwest corner of the corral and was caused by "Nosey Kate's" tent being very close to the corral wall. N.K. has a reputation of her own, and when I

TOMBSTONE AND "CACHISE" COUNTY, 1881

Many of the early maps can't make up their minds about the spelling of the Chiricahua's chief's name. This is an example of one, before it was finally changed to Cochise County.

This is the arroyo where Curly Bill shoots Marshal White

inquired who she was, everybody looked blank. She had a lot of fellows about the premises always drunk, sometimes disorderly, carousing and drinking, and they were cooking, as they usually did, by an open fire, and a little breeze did the balance." (The "Nosey Kate" in this article is not "Big Nose Kate." In fact, the two have been confused for a long time. See page 40.)

Summer, 1880

Morgan and his common-law wife Lou arrive in Tombstone to join the other Earp brothers and set down roots.

The Earps have been renting an adobe shack (for $45 a month) on Allen Street until they can build their own homes. James has a job as a bartender at Vogans. Virgil is a U.S. Deputy Marshal and Wyatt settled for a job as a Wells Fargo messenger guard—salary, $125 a month (he originally came to Tombstone intending to quit "lawing" and start his own stage line, but there were already two stage companies up and running when he arrived). The Earp women have been sewing canvas tents to bring in extra money.

July, 1880

The sheriff of Pima County, Charles Shibell, reports to the Board of Supervisors that the assessed valuation of houses and improvements in Tombstone is $125,455 and personal property is valued at $87,455.

Ike Clanton briefly opens a restaurant in Watervale, just outside Tombstone. He also finds time to unload $2,000 worth of cattle of "suspicious origin" on the beef contractor at the San Carlos Apache Reservation. With Ike are Joe Hill—alias "King Pin," Dutch George and another unknown cow-boy. After the sale, the quartet leaves San Carlos and rides up the Gila River "shooting into every house they ride by."

"Doc received a letter from Wyatt Earp stating that Tombstone was very lively and that Doc could do well there as there was no dentists there."
—BIG NOSE KATE

Tombstone, looking east from Comstock Hill, 1879. Compare this photo with the view on page 69, taken two years later. (ARIZONA HISTORICAL SOCIETY)

BURNING THE MIDNIGHT OIL
When Doc arrives in Tombstone, there is no record of him practicing dentistry at all. Instead he gambles full-time, often with Kate standing over his shoulder. The two of them are inseparable for periods of time. Other times they need to be separated.

THE MARSHAL WHITE SHOOTING
The debate over Curly Bill's "accidental" shooting continues to this day.

July 25, 1880

U.S. Deputy Marshal Virgil Earp deputizes Wyatt and Morgan to help locate six army mules taken from Camp Rucker. The animals are located at the ranch of Frank and Tom McLaury. This first clash with "cow-boys" results in a festering enmity between the Earps and McLaurys.

July 27, 1880

Wyatt Earp accepts the appointment by Sheriff Charles Shibell as deputy sheriff for the Tombstone district of Pima County. Earp is the first county officer of recognized standing in Tombstone. Shibell's first priority is for Earp to start collecting taxes on the burgeoning mining district. Wyatt will turn his shotgun messenger job over to Morgan.

Late August-Early September, 1880

Dr. and Mrs. Holliday leave Prescott heading for the boom camp of Tombstone, but enroute Kate decides she doesn't want to go there. She says to Doc: "If you are going to tie yourself to the Earp Brothers, go to it. I am going to Globe." The two travel on to Gillette where there are no accommodations for the night. Doc and Kate finally persuade the mine superintendent to give them a bed in his office. Years later Kate remembered that, "It was a good bed too. There was a store there, and we had a kind of a breakfast next morning. We started out again, Doc to Tombstone and I to Globe." There is contradicting evidence about Kate going to Globe at this point. When Doc is implicated in the killing of Philpot, the July 6, 1881 Tombstone *Nugget* reports that, "The warrant was issued upon the affidavit of Kate Elder with whom Holliday has been living for some time past."

Doc Holliday, the living dead man, arrives in Tombstone. Never have a municipality and a man been better suited to each other. Holliday's consumption is acting up and every night is a walk across hell on a spider's web. When every cough requires a swig of whiskey, the world seems especially ripe for contempt.

September, 1880

Wyatt becomes secretary of the Tombstone Volunteer Fire Company. Meanwhile, the Earp houses are almost complete *(see photo, page 69).*

Doctor George E. Goodfellow resigns from the U.S. Army and arrives in Tombstone determined to open a hospital.

Virgil Earp is appointed assistant marshal of the village of Tombstone. His salary is $100 a month.

The popular Oriental saloon is being high-pressured by Johnny Tyler, a professional gambler with a reputation, into taking him into partnership in the gambling room. Tyler, with the aid of his friends, is keeping the Oriental in a constant uproar, starting fights, getting loud, scaring away the more genteel gamblers, rattling the faro dealers with a string of obscene comments, and generally behaving like a goober.

Lou Rickabough, the owner of the Oriental's gambling concession, finally has enough, and hires Wyatt Earp—for one-quarter interest—to protect the Oriental from thugs. Earp's method is straightforward. He walks up to Tyler, slaps him silly and hauls him out the swinging doors by his earlobe. The carpets aren't even tainted by a drop of blood.

September 27, 1880

J.H. Holliday, dentist, registers to vote in Pima County, District 17 (the village of Tombstone). This is the first documented presence of Doc Holliday in Tombstone.

On The Town

Kate walks arm in arm with her man after taking in a performance at Schieffelin Hall. They are returning to their room at Fly's lodging house. Oil lights, light the main intersections as well as the saloons.

"I went in to see once where he was with another woman. I had a big knife with me and said I'd rip her open... [Doc] came away from her."
—BIG NOSE KATE

THE JOYCE SHOOTING
Doc enters with a bang.

October, 1880

Johnny Behan moves to Tombstone from Tip Top (near Prescott). With him is his son, Albert. Recently divorced and a notorious wencher, Behan has taken up with a beautiful actress named Josephine Sarah Marcus, whom he had impressed when she performed in Prescott. The 18-year-old Josephine lives in Tombstone with Behan as his wife. Tradition says that when she arrived on the stage, the shotgun messenger, Morgan Earp, greeted his older brother Wyatt, and that this was Josephine and Wyatt's first meeting.

October 11, 1880

Within weeks of arriving in Tombstone, Doc Holliday gets in a shooting scrape at the Oriental saloon. Johnny Tyler, the very same gambler who Wyatt Earp eighty-sixed last month, has hot words with Doc. Flashing his infamous temper, Holliday challenges, goads and taunts Tyler to pull his shooter. Showing rare good sense, Tyler declines to fight a man who wants to die. Shamed, the tinhorn leaves camp, but Milt Joyce, the owner of the Oriental, takes Holliday to task for his wanton blood lust. As Joyce continues to rail against Doc (the dentist gave up his pistol to Joyce, which is now safely deposited behind the bar), the good doctor gets madder and madder. Finally, Holliday can take no more abuse and he bolts out the front door, obtains another pistol and returns.

The Tombstone *Nugget* reports that: "[Holliday] walked toward Joyce, who was just coming from behind the bar, and with a remark that would not look good in print, turned loose with a self-cocker. Joyce was not more than ten feet away and jumped for his assailant and struck him over the head with a six-shooter, felling him to the floor and lighting on top of him. Officers White and Bennett were near at hand and separated them, taking the pistols from each. Just how many shots were fired none present seemed able to tell but in casting up accounts Joyce was found to be shot through the hand, his partner, Mr. Parker, who was behind the bar, shot through the big toe of the left foot, and Holliday with a blow of the pistol in Joyce's hands."

October 12, 1880

In custody of Fred White, Holliday is brought before Justice of the Peace James Reilly. Doc is offered a plea of assault and battery, which is accepted. He is sentenced and fined $20, plus court costs of $11. (Holliday won't pay this fine until December 15, which would seem to deflate the claim that Doc amassed a $10,000 poke in Prescott.)

October 28, 1880

A half-hour past midnight, three or four pistol shots are heard coming from an arroyo just off Allen Street in downtown Tombstone. When a small crowd, including Wyatt and Morgan Earp, run down to investigate, they discover a group of cow-boys shooting at the moon. City Marshal Fred White is the first one on the scene and he confronts the apparent leader, Curly Bill Brocius, and demands his six-shooter. As Wyatt Earp runs up and grabs Bill from behind, White grabs hold of the cow-boy's gun barrel and barks, "Now give me that God-damned gun you son-of-a-bitch." As he does so, the gun discharges, striking White in the left testicle. Wyatt buffaloes Curly Bill with a borrowed pistol and most of the cow-boys are rounded up and put in the small (12' by 12' wooden plank) makeshift jail, which is literally a stone's throw away from the shooting.

October 29, 1880

City Marshal White gives a

WAS DOC HOLLIDAY A LOUSY SHOT?

Drunk or sober, Doc Holliday was willing.

Several writers have made light of Doc Holliday's "poor marksmanship." They point out his statistical shot sheet like he was a cleanup hitter. "He shot at seven men, only hitting two, for a measly .250 average. I'm sorry, but that's not quite good enough for the majors..." This is very misleading (because he was good enough for the majors!). As the old saying goes, there are lies, and there are damn lies and then there are statistics. First of all, we can't even accurately list the number of men he shot at. For example, Wyatt Earp claimed Doc killed Ed Bailey in Texas, but there is no record of it. Bat Masterson claimed that Doc shot another man in Colorado, but once again, no document exists to prove it. Also, what was Holliday's part in the shooting of Frank Stillwell and Florentino? No proof. No hits. No runs No errors.

Finally, and most importantly, we don't know Doc's intent—was he shooting to scare, shooting to mame, or shooting to kill? Maybe he "missed" on purpose. What we do know is—*he was willing.* Any man who went up against Doc Holliday knew one thing: he didn't care. He *wanted* to die. If death wasn't a certainty when he stands against you, neither is life. Who wants to take that chance? Evidently, not many.

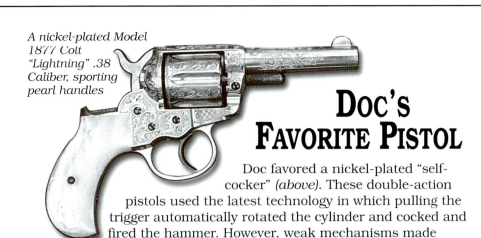

A nickel-plated Model 1877 Colt "Lightning" .38 Caliber, sporting pearl handles

DOC'S FAVORITE PISTOL

Doc favored a nickel-plated "self-cocker" *(above)*. These double-action pistols used the latest technology in which pulling the trigger automatically rotated the cylinder and cocked and fired the hammer. However, weak mechanisms made them less reliable than single action guns. This was in contrast to the "old" single-action revolvers *(below)* which required two movements to fire—cocking the hammer with the thumb which rotated the cylinder, and then pulling the trigger. The irony is that a "double-action" pistol requires only one action, while the "single-action" requires two actions (the action refers to the gun's mechanism, not the user's.) To make matters even more confusing, the gunfighters used "black powder," which emitted white smoke. Son of a gun.

A SINGLE-ACTION IN ACTION

Grabbing the hammer by the thumb and pulling back (below), *the shooter reaches three stops. The first is a safety, which prevents accidental firing. However, this might result in the gun going off anyway because the mechanism was weak and often broke. The second stop, or "half-cock" is for loading and unloading, but would often slip and cause accidental discharge hence the term "half-cocked." The third, or "full-cock," is ready for firing.*

MAKING HASTE SLOWLY

The gunfighters who preferred the single-action Colt needed to pull the revolver from its holster, cock it, aim and pull the trigger. A very cumbersome process and one that makes the gunfighters speed and accuracy even more incredible.

Colt S.A. .44 —.40 Cal. with 7 1/2 inch barrel
(ABE HAYS, ARIZONA WEST GALLERY)

SAMUEL COLT

THE FATHER AND THE SON (OF A GUN)

Samuel Colt hated the double-action revolver. He claimed that firing the damn thing with accuracy was impossible, because of the force necessary to pull the trigger. Fifteen years after Colt's death the company he founded came out with the double-action Lightning Model of 1877. Doc Holliday, Billy the Kid and Pat Garrett all disagreed with Samuel Colt and carried double-action Colts.

statement, under oath, that exonerates Curly Bill, stating the shooting was an accident. Still, rumors circulate that a lynch mob is going to take Curly Bill from the jail, so a buggy is brought up and Wyatt Earp takes the reins and delivers Brocius to Tucson for safe-keeping.

October 30, 1880
Marshal White's condition worsens and he dies. Ben Sippy is appointed to replace White.

November 9, 1880
A lifelong Republican, Wyatt resigns his deputy sheriff position to support Bob Paul's campaign for Pima County Sheriff. Johnny Behan is named to replace Earp.

November 12, 1880
In the election, the cow-boys strongly back the incumbent Democrat, Charles Shibell. In the heart of cow-boy turf—the San Simon district—Johnny Ringo serves as precinct judge and Ike Clanton is a voting inspector. To the shock and disgust of county Republicans, Curly Bill (out on bail) rides into Tombstone with the San Simon returns: 103 votes for Chas. Shibell, one for Bob Paul.

The San Simon vote swings the election to Shibell and Paul immediately contests the results.

In the election for Tombstone City Marshal, Ben Sippy beats Virgil Earp, 311 votes to 259.

November 15, 1880
Irritated, Virgil Earp resigns as assistant marshal.

Late 1880
After the Milt Joyce set-to, Doc leads an unusually quiet life in Tombstone. The November 1880, *Nugget* notes a telegram for him is awaiting pick up. Even when Marshal White is killed by Curly Bill in October, there is no mention of Doc taking part in the Earp's round up of cow-boys that night.

Mid-December, 1880

Curly Bill's trial for the killing of Marshal White is postponed until January. Wyatt visits Curly Bill and makes a proposal: If the cowboy will identify the ballot box-stuffers in the San Simon district, Wyatt and Morgan will testify the White shooting was accidental. Brocius thinks it over and agrees. He accuses Ike Clanton of voter fraud.

Wyatt rides to Charleston. Acting on a tip from Sherm McMasters, a member of the cowboys who actually was a double-agent, Earp learns that his stolen horse "Dick Naylor" can be found at the mill town on the San Pedro. Doc and Wyatt find his prize race horse being ridden by Billy Clanton. After a tense standoff, young Clanton removes his saddle and Wyatt retrieves his horse.

During the Yuletide holiday, both Wyatt and Virgil enter horses in the Christmas Trotter Race being held in Tombstone.

December 29, 1880

John Clum is named Republican candidate for Mayor.

January, 1881

Wyatt and Morgan Earp travel to Tucson and testify in the Curly Bill murder trial that the shooting of Marshal White was an accident. Wyatt even takes the jury out back and shows them how the gun could easily have been discharged.

Curly Bill Brocius is found not guilty.

January 4, 1881

John Clum wins his bid to become mayor of Tombstone, 532 votes to 165.

January 8, 1881

Celebrating the release of Curly Bill, the cow-boys and their captain shoot up Charleston and break up a religious meeting, making the preacher "dance."

THE OTHER WOMAN

Styles of attractiveness change over time. One epoch's heartthrob may leave the next generation cold. By all accounts, Josephine Sarah Marcus was a shinning beauty to her time. Bat Masterson claimed she was the best-looking woman within a three-hundred-mile radius of Tombstone. One newspaper, in the 1880s made a point of describing Josie as a "lady anywhere." But what was considered beautiful in 1880? A clue might be gained by studying the image of a well-known actress who gained equal praise for her appeal. Jeffreys Lewis was a raven-haired New York performer who inspired much the same praise as did Josephine Marcus. Here is the type of beauty the 1880s admired.

While in Tombstone, Josephine lived openly as Mrs. Johnny Behan, a prized possession of Wyatt Earp's most adamant rival. Rumors persist, however, that she worked as a prostitute while in the silver camp. The most surprising implication that such was the case came from Doc Holliday. In 1882, Doc told Denver reporters about an argument he'd had with Johnny Behan. "In the quarrel I told him in presence of a crowd that he (Johnny) was gambling with money which I had given his woman. This story got out and caused him trouble." Was Doc impugning Josephine's honor? That's hard to say. Behan wasn't a one-women man. So, while Doc's comment is provocative it's far from conclusive. Josephine could have merely been "free-spirited," which would have raised eyebrows in those Victorian times. It's doubtful, however, she was ever "on the line" as a professional. She was a "lady anywhere."

JEFFREYS LEWIS

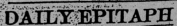

DAILY EPITAPH

OFFICIAL JOURNAL OF TOMBSTONE.

FRIDAY MORNING, - - - JULY 29, 1881.

LOCAL SPLINTERS.

THE mills on the river will start up work again to-day.

JUDGE SMITH will resume his reply to the Hon. Thomas Fitch this morning at 9 o'clock.

THESE passengers left by Sandy Bob's stage to-day: B Brana, P Pielean, Mr Brewislen.

READ the synopsis of Hon. Thomas Fitch's great argument on the railroad case, which appears in this issue.

THE following unclaimed telegrams remain at the Western Union office: F Farnsworth, H M Cox, George Waugh, H M Kingsbury.

THE accordeon fiend will take this notice as final, and will be ready to die at sunrise. We hate to do it, but life is just as sweet to us as it is to him.

AMONG the annoyances caused by the late heavy rains to the business men of Tombstone the deprivation of mails since Tuesday has not been the least.

THE following passengers left by Kinnear's line to-day: Mrs Behan, A Goodman, Jas Young, E S Armstrong, J F Saw, Chas Ziemer, J H Murray, A C Cowan.

AT the Grand: Geo F Prance; A J Moore, San Francisco; C W Barker, Tucson; B L Conyers, Phoenix; W B Rich, San Francisco; M L Drew, A S Hopkins, Sacramento.

ONE day last week, in going from Pantano to Harshaw, Ingram & Co's stage, while passing through a canyon during a storm, was upset by the water and lost the mail and one horse drowned.

AT the Cosmopolitan: M D Clement, San Francisco; C M Burker, John McGonigle, Tucson; F Moffett, Charleston; John K Ross Bodie; Joseph Young, Contention; D B Reid, M D Leslee, Tucson; Geo S Barber, Charleston.

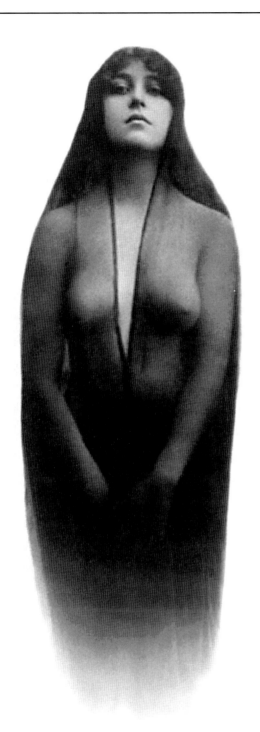

THE INFAMOUS NUDE PHOTO

By now everyone in America is aware of the alleged nude photo of Josephine. (In fact, both recent Wyatt Earp movies had scenes about this photo.) It is not her. The photograph has been tracked to the ABC Novelty Company, in Brooklyn, New York. It has a copyright date of 1914 and in fact, if you look closely, it is not even an 1880s-style photograph. It's been widely reproduced on naughty Mexican postcards and even as a Vanilla Fudge rock poster in the sixties.

January 9, 1881

Still on a drunken spree, Curly Bill and his cow-boy comrades take their "jollification" on the road and, arriving in Tombstone, shoot up the inside of the Alhambra Saloon and race their horses down Allen Street shooting and "hurrahing" the town.

January 14, 1881

An 18-year-old tough, Johnny O'Rourke, shoots and kills mining engineer W. P. Schneider in Charleston. As a lynch mob forms, the local constable loads his prisoner, alias Johnny-Behind-The-Deuce, in a wagon and makes a dash towards Tombstone. Just as the mob is about to overtake them, Virgil Earp rides up (he's out exercising Wyatt's horse, Dick Naylor) and the constable gladly unloads his prisoner. Without much persuasion, Johnny jumps up behind Virgil, and the two make tracks to Tombstone in record time. It is here that Wyatt Earp holds off the angry crowd of miners with a shotgun, while Virgil, Ben Sippy and Johnny Behan get a wagon to take the young defendant to Tucson.

On the very same day of the Johnny-Behind-The-Deuce affair, "Buckskin" Frank Leslie orders a special 12-inch-barreled six-shooter from the Colt factory. (It is speculated that perhaps he was inspired by seeing a similar gun on the person of Wyatt Earp.)

February 1, 1881

Cochise County (originally spelled "Cachise" see map, page 28) is created out of Pima County with Tombstone as the county seat. Johnny Behan is appointed the first sheriff of the new county. Behan names Harry Woods, editor of the *Nugget*, as his under-sheriff and appoints Dave Campbell, Dave Neagle, Frank Stillwell, Lance Perkins, Frank Hereford and Billy Breakenridge as his deputies.

February 5, 1881

The tiny town of Phoenix is incorporated.

Doc Holliday resumes a quiet lifestyle. One of his better friends is Billy Leonard, a jeweler Holliday met in Las Vegas, New Mexico. Billy is also consumptive so a bond of sympathy and mutual misery connect the two. According to Stuart Lake, Holliday disapproves of some of Leonard's friends; Luther King, Harry Head and Jim Crane, all members of the cow-boy gang. Leonard is recruited by the outlaws to use his skills to help melt down stolen jewelry from robberies pulled by the cow-boy crowd.

February 25, 1881

LUKE SHORT

Fresh from Dodge City, Bat Masterson and Luke Short blow into town to sample the waters. A rowdy cow-boy, Charlie Storms, tries to mix it up with one of the Dodge City boys and is shot down in front of the Oriental Saloon by Luke Short. Less than a week later, a man named McAllister shoots and kills "One-Armed Kelly" in the Oriental and an embattled Milt Joyce closes the game room. George Parsons writes in his journal: "Oriental a regular slaughterhouse now."

March 15, 1881

At night, an attempt is made to rob the Kinnear Stage. Eli 'Budd' Philpot is the driver and Bob Paul acts as shotgun messenger. The coach is an old one that has already seen thirty years' service over creek and gully in California before 'Sandy Bob' Crouch brought it to Tombstone in 1880 for the Benson run. It is a cold, damp night, having snowed this morning. The air is clear and a

Luke Short Photo (**COURTESY KANSAS STATE HISTORICAL SOCIETY**)

THE PRIZED MINORITY

"The ladies of Tombstone are not so liberally provided with entertainment, and find little enjoyment aside from a stroll about town after sunset, the only comfortable time of the day. The camp is one of the dirtiest places in the world, When black garments appear to have been laid away in an old barrel, and one is never sure of having a clean face, despite repeated ablutions, it is time to talk about dirt."

—Clara Spalding Brown, writing to the *San Diego Union.*

ELIZABETH CHANEY

Going for a horseback ride is one of the activities that women can enjoy, as long as they don't mind the dirt. (ARIZONA HISTORICAL SOCIETY LIBRARY)

THE SINGLES SCENE

MARY ALVORD
*She's available but her brother is
Burt Alvord, the train robber.*
(ARIZONA HISTORICAL SOCIETY LIBRARY)

CORA VIOLA HOWELL
*She's one of the most sought after
females in Arizona, but watch out
for her boyfriend, Texas John
Slaughter.*

A DISCUSSION ON WOMAN'S RIGHTS.

Algernon (to his Sisters, his Cousins, and his Aunts). "MY DEAR CREATURES, IF YOU WANT EQUALITY AMONG THE SEXES, YOU MUST LEARN TO BE INDEPENDENT OF US, AS WE ARE OF YOU. NOW WE MEN LIVE CHIEFLY TO PLEASE OURSELVES FIRST, AND THEN EACH OTHER; WHEREAS YOU WOMEN LIVE ENTIRELY TO PLEASE *Us!*"

*Punch, (above) The English Humor Publication was available in Tombstone
along with all the latest magazines from the States.*

near full moon hangs skull-like in the starry night sky.

Some question exists whether Paul and Philpot exchange places because 'Budd' is experiencing some kind of stomach distress. None of the initial reports of the robbery attempt make mention of such a switch. First mention appearing in the Aug. 25 *Nugget*, which credits the story to one of the robbers himself, Jim Crane.

Apparently the robbers wait a few miles east of Contention City. There they eyeball the coach as it lumbers along. If there is a guard, they know the coach carries treasure and they ride pell-mell cross country to wait in ambush above Contention near Drews Station.

Finally as the coach creaks up a sharp incline out from a dry wash, a voice comes from the dark, "Hold." Instantly Paul sizes up the situation and barks back, "By God, I halt for no one!" He puts his shotgun to his shoulder and lets loose. The bandits blast back, hitting Philpot, who tumbles off the coach and killing passenger Peter Roerig who is unlucky enough to be riding on the dickey seat up top.

The coach careens wildly up the road out of control and past Drews Station. The reins fall out of reach and it takes Bob Paul a wild mile before he can stop the coach, retrieve the reins and proceed on to Benson. Once there, Paul wires Tombstone. Ready men respond and the hunt is on.

A posse with Behan, the Earps and Bat Masterson pursues the robbers for seventeen days. Their only catch, Luther King, is sent back to Tombstone only to walk out from Under-sheriff Harry Woods' less-than-vigilant, restraint. When the Earps, return the town is abuzz with suspicion of Doc Holliday's involvement.

The *Tucson Star* wrote: "This party (Doc) is suspected for the reason that on the afternoon of the attack, he engaged a horse at a Tombstone livery stable at about

THE WEST IS WILD...
BUT THE WOMEN ARE WILDER!

PAULINE MARKHAM
This stunning beauty is showing quite a bit of leg for the 1880s, and what a pair of gams! Her "Pinafore on Wheels" dance troupe tours the west, and it is Pauline who brings Josephine Sarah Marcus to Tombstone.

DUTCH ANNIE
A successful madame, she runs one of the largest whore houses in Tombstone.
(ARIZONA HISTORICAL SOCIETY LIBRARY)

NOSEY KATE
A prostitute in Tombstone. She established Tombstone's first dance hall in a tent. For years she has been mistakenly identified as Big Nose Kate. They were two separate whores.

BIG MINNIE
The wife of Joe Bignon, owner and manager of the Bird Cage Theater. Over two hundred and thirty pounds of entertainment goes a long way, especially in tights.

THE ILLUSTRATED LIFE AND TIMES OF DOC HOLLIDAY 41

LIZETTE, THE FLYING NYMPH
She soars over the stage for the Monarch Carnival Company.

HONEST WOMEN

"Saloon openings are all the rage. 'The Oriental' is simply gorgeous and is pronounced the finest place of the kind this side of San Francisco. The bar is a marvel of beauty; the sideboards were made for the Baldwin Hotel; the gaming room connected with Brussels, brilliantly lighted, and furnished with reading matter and writing materials for its patrons. Every evening music from a piano and the violin attracts a crowd; and the singing is really a gay one—but all for the men. To be sure, there are frequent dances, which I have heard called "respectable;" but as long as so many members of the demi-monde, who are very numerous and very showy here, patronize them, many honest women will hesitate to attend."

—Clara Spalding Brown, August 3, 1880, writing to the *San Diego Union*

4 o'clock, stating that he might be gone for 7 or 8 days and he might return that night, and picked the best animal in the stable. He left town about 4 o'clock armed with a Henry rifle and a six-shooter, he started toward Charleston, and about a mile below Tombstone cut across to Contention, and when next seen it was between 10 and 11 o'clock riding into the livery stable at Tombstone, his horse fagged out. He at once called for another horse, which he hitched in the streets for some hours, but did not leave. Statements attributed to him, if true, looks very bad indeed and which, if proven, are most conclusive as to his guilt either as a principle actor or as an accessory before the fact."

Doc's story is that he'd heard of a big game in Charleston, and rode over that afternoon. Of course he was armed, only a dammed fool would traipse around the country without the means for self-protection. When he arrived at Charleston the game was over so he returned, hitching his horse behind Old Man Fullers water wagon and riding back with Fuller. He said he was back in town by 6 p.m. and spent the night gambling at the Alhambra.

April-June, 1881

Again a low profile for Holliday. Fed up with rumors of his involvement in the Benson stage robbery, Doc issues a general threat that he'll kill the next person to utter such slander.

"If I had pulled that job, I'd have got the eighty thousand."
—DOC HOLLIDAY,
AS QUOTED BY STUART LAKE, IN
FRONTIER MARSHAL

April 16, 1881

In Tombstone for a mere two months, Bat Masterson returns to Dodge City to aid his brother, Marshal Jim Masterson who is embroiled in a political feud. Bat gets off the train, in Dodge, and starts shooting at his brother's enemies. Both Mastersons are asked to leave town and they do.

May, 1881

Curly Bill Brocius is shot in the face by Jim Wallace during a wild drinking spree in Galeyville. The bullet hits the Captain of the Rustlers in the cheek, knocks out a tooth and exits through his neck. In spite of the serious wound, Curly Bill recovers. Many in Tombstone are sorry that Wallace is such a lousy shot. In late May, the murder case against Luke Short in the Storms killing is dismissed. Short leaves Arizona for good.

June, 1881

Marshal Ben Sippy leaves town under a cloud (it is later speculated that he was trying to avoid paying off substantial debts). Virgil Earp is appointed marshal in his stead. One of Virgil's first acts is to arrest his brother, Wyatt, for fighting and disturbing the peace (he will also arrest Mayor Clum for riding his horse too fast within the city limits).

June 22, 1881

A whiskey barrel in front of the Arcade Saloon explodes when a bartender lights a match to look inside, and the Tombstone business center is devastated by another fire. Losses are estimated from $175,000 to $300,000.

Late June-Early July, 1881

After a bitter argument Kate decides to get even with her man. Johnny Behan gets Kate drunk and coaxes her into signing a piece of paper—that claims Doc was indeed involved in the Benson stage robbery.

CHARLESTON, 1880

A rare photo of the milling town on the San Pedro where the cow-boys rule when they aren't at Galeyville. It is here that Wyatt will retrieve his stolen horse, Dick Naylor, from Billy Clanton. An Ore wagon (below) *laden with silver ore leaves the mines for Charleston.*

WYATT EARP

There is no love lost between Kate and Wyatt (see pullquote below). She isn't alone. Virgil's wife, Allie, has her problems with the "saloon keeper," not to mention Wyatt's common-law wife, Mattie, who commits suicide in 1888, over his desertion.

"'You say the word and I'll leave Tombstone,' Doc told Wyatt, as they left the courtroom. 'You send that fool woman away and I'll be satisfied,' Wyatt answered."

—STUART LAKE,
IN *FRONTIER MARSHAL*, 1928

KATE PLOTS REVENGE (BBB)

"Important Arrest

A warrant was sworn out yesterday before Judge Spicer for the arrest of Doc Holliday, a well-known character here, charging him with complicity in the murder of Budd Philpot, and the attempted stage robbery near Contention some months ago, and he was arrested by Sheriff Behan. The warrant was issued upon the affidavit of Kate Elder, with whom Holliday had been living for some time past."

The rivalry between Johnny Behan and Wyatt Earp is already a rough and tumble political brawl. The Benson stage robbery attempt focuses the tension. In June, Wyatt enlists Ike Clanton to get Leonard, Head and Crane—the trio of robbers widely thought to have attempted the heist.

Earp and Clanton's unholy alliance produces nothing as Leonard and Head are killed by the Hazlett brothers in New Mexico. Meanwhile Ike Clanton is plagued by demons. Though nothing results from his deal with Wyatt, he grows nervous that Earp is talking of their arrangement. Wells Fargo Agent

Marshal Williams figures what's up when Earp wires the home office about reward money. One night a drunk Williams foolishly assures Clanton that any deal Ike has with Wyatt is just fine with him. Stunned, Ike's suspicions grow feverish.

July 14, 1881

In a darkened bedroom at Fort Sumner, New Mexico, Billy the Kid is shot dead by Pat Garrett. The kid's last words are— "¿Quien es?" (Who is it?)

July 20, 1881

The *Las Vegas Optic* gloats about Doc's latest troubles: "It will be remembered, especially by the pioneers of the East Side, that Doc Holliday was at one time the keeper of a gin-mill on Centre Street, near the present site of the Centre Street bakery. Doc was always considered a shiftless, bagged-legged character—a killer and professional cut-throat and not a whit too refined to rob stages or even steal sheep. He is the identical individual who killed poor, inoffensive Mike Gordon and crept through one of the many legal loop-holes that characterized Hoodoo Brown's judicial dispensation."

August, 1881

OLD MAN CLANTON
(B.B.B.)

Old Man Clanton, Dixie Gray and the last surviving member of the Benson stage robbers—Jim Crane—are ambushed and killed with others in Guadalupe Canyon near the Mexican line. Mexican soldiers are believed to have been the ambushers, and

COLONEL GOMEZ, ON THE BORDER WITH CROOKS
A Mexican officer who fought smugglers, rustlers and Apaches along the boundary-line in the eighties. Colonel Gomez is a friend of Texas John Slaughter.
(ARIZONA HISTORICAL SOCIETY LIBRARY)

OLD MAN CLANTON GETS HIS
Cow-boy rustlers headed by Old Man Clanton (below) raid Mexico one too many times. They will be ambushed in Guadalupe Canyon and will pay for their sins.

Fly's Gallery, *Just from The Indian Country* *Sonora - Mexico.* Tombstone, A. T.

GEORGE PARSONS, 1881
Parsons keeps a daily journal for most of his life and his Tombstone entries are a remarkable insight into the daily life of that community. He also spends time in Sonora prospecting for mines and the photo (above) is taken when he returns. It may appear to be a joke, or overkill, but most travelers along the border arm themselves just as heavily as Parsons is, and they never regret it.

allegedly were retaliating against a cow-boy ambush and massacre of a Mexican supply train in Skeleton Canyon the previous month.

September, 1881
One of two suspects wanted in a February stage holdup near Globe is spotted in Tombstone. His name is Sherm McMasters. Virgil Earp wires Sheriff Bob Paul in Tucson to confirm McMasters "wanted" status. Meanwhile, McMasters spooks and makes for his horse. Virgil Earp steps into the middle of the street and lets loose with five shots at the fleeing McMasters, all of which miss. This is considered peculiar because Virgil Earp had earlier won a rifle shooting contest in Tombstone and is considered a crack shot. Many felt he missed on purpose. In fact, he has. But not for the reasons being circulated—that the Earps are in cahoots with the stage robbers. McMasters is an undercover infiltrator working for Wells Fargo. A fact Earp knows but can't publicly explain.

THE MEXICAN VAQUERO
The American cow-boy owes plenty to his Mexican cousins. The language, the style of dress, the equipment and most of the herds heading for market come from south of the border.

THE COW-BOY CONSPIRACY?

Look hard at the faces of the men around the branding fire on the opposite page. Do they look like a cunning gang of conspirators?

Hardly. Now look at the faces of the cow-boys to the right. Do they look like a cunning gang of conspirators? Maybe. One thing is clear, when you study these cow-boys it's easy to understand Big Nose Kate's observation that it's foolish to think country gun-men can go up against city gun-men.

Granted, the cow-boys in Arizona during the eighties were a tough lot. Local rancher Henry Clay Hooker said, "We take a man here and ask no questions. We know when he throws a saddle on his horse whether he understands his business or not. He may be a minister back-slidin', or a banker savin' his last lung, or a train robber on a vacation—we don't care. A good many of our most useful men have made their mistakes. All we care about is, will they stand the gaff? Will they sit sixty hours in the saddle, holdin' a herd that's tryin' to stampede all the time?"

Unlike the Earps and Holliday, many of these stockmen stayed on to settle and raise families in Cochise County. To this day, one can travel the back roads and visit the descendants of the "dreaded Cow-Boys" and wonder if there is any relationship between them and the so-called evil Cow-Boy Gang.

And not surprisingly, today's ranchers have few kind words for Doc Holliday or his friends.

IKE CLANTON

BILLY CLANTON

TOM MCLAURY

FRANK MCLAURY

BRANDING TIME AT THE LOWRY RANCH, NEAR TOMBSTONE, 1883
An excellent sampling of cow-boy gear is on display in these two sequential photographs. Note the Mexican sugarloaf hat on the mounted vaquero, right center, in the photo above. (ARIZONA HISTORICAL SOCIETY)

DOC'S SYMPTOMS

"I said to him one day: 'Doctor, don't your conscience ever trouble you?' 'No,' he replied, with that peculiar cough of his, 'I coughed that up with my lungs long ago.'"
—COL. JOHN T. DEWEESE

Consumption can go undetected for some good time, especially if the tendency towards denial is followed. Fatigue is more and more pronounced as one's appetite seems to disappear. One feels 'out of sorts' and clammy. Periods of fever come and go. One wakes up in the dead of night drenched in sweat. In the morning, choking, coughing and spitting up, at first watery fluid, later blood and chunks of lung tissue, rack the sufferer. The chest feels as if it were imploding and the pain of it all leads many to alcohol for temporary respite. To crown it all, many thought the illness a result of moral laxity. Compounded with terror of contagion, the consumptive becomes something of a pariah—a "lunger" despised in and for his infirmity.

The disease may be acute or chronic and generally attacks the respiratory tract, although any tissue may be affected. The symptoms (fever, loss of weight, etc.) are caused by the toxins produced by the infecting organism, which also cause the formation of characteristic nodes consisting of a packed mass of cells and dead tissue.

LOTTIE DENO

"Why you low-down slinking slut! If I should step in soft cow manure, I would not even clean my foot on that bastard!"
—LOTTIE DENO

RESPONDING TO BIG NOSE KATE'S ACCUSATION THAT LOTTIE WAS TRYING TO STEAL HER MAN

THOSE WHO KNEW DOC DESCRIBE HIM

"Holliday had few real friends any-where in the West. He was selfish and had a perverse nature—traits not calculated to make a man popular in the early days on the frontier."
 —Bat Masterson

"He never boasted of his fighting qualities. He was a neat dresser, and saw to it his wife was dressed as nicely as himself."
 —Kate

"The doctor was a peculiar one and deceptive in his methods. He would seem to backout and hesitate as if afraid, then suddenly he would rush on his antagonist and before the latter knew what was coming he would be laid out stiff with one of the doctor's bullets in his carcass."
 —Col. John T. Deweese, Attorney

"Doc Holliday was a native of Georgia and take him all in all, he was possessed of the most daredevil and reckless bravery of any of his associates."
 —C.P. Thomas, plainsman,
 in the *Washington Post*, 1906

"[Doc was] close to six feet tall, weight—one hundred and sixty pounds, fair complexion, very pretty mustache, blue-grey eyes, and a fine set of teeth."
 —Kate

September 8, 1881
 The Tombstone-Bisbee stage is held up near Hereford and robbed of twenty-five hundred dollars in the Wells-Fargo box and a mail sack. Jewelry and seven-hundred and fifty dollars in currency are taken from four passengers. There is no shotgun messenger on the stage and the driver, Levi McDaniels, offers no resistance. One of the two masked robbers keeps saying, "Give up the sugar," and "Don't hide any sugar from us." In spite of the mask, McDaniel's recognizes the "sugar" man as Frank Stillwell, one of Johnny Behan's deputies. He also recognizes the other road agent as Peter Spencer. Off in the chaparral are two other accomplices, but incredibly McDaniels cannot identify them.

September 20, 1881
 President James A. Garfield dies from gunshot wounds he received on July 2. Tombstone goes into mourning and riders adorn their saddle pommels with black crape paper.

JOHN CLUM

October 4, 1881
 Whistles blow and armed squads run through the streets of Tombstone as word reaches the silver camp of a fight with Apaches in South Pass, a mere 16 miles away. At noon a large party forms

The Palace Hotel in Tucson
Note the Tombstone stage line (below), and the amenities, including telephones in the above ad.

CHARLIE SHIBELL
The early sheriff of Pima County who makes Wyatt Earp his deputy. Shibell looses his post to Bob Paul after the contested election of 1880 was overturned in April 1881.

DID WYATT EARP USE A TELEPHONE IN TOMBSTONE?

"Hello! Hello! Hello! is that you, Wyatt?"

In 1926, Wyatt Earp wrote his autobiography with a friend, John Flood. In it he recalled using a telephone in Tombstone, on March 15, 1881. Could that be possible? We know that a phone system was being discussed for Tombstone in April of 1881, and that phones were advertised in Tucson hotels by 1882 (see add on opposite page). John Clum remembered using a telephone to call Tombstone from one of the mines in December of 1881. However, long distance lines to Benson (where Wyatt claimed the call originated from) in March of '81 seems improbable and newspaper accounts of the robbery attempt are uniform in saying, Virgil Earp was sent a telegram. In spite of that, it's interesting that Wyatt would remember using a telephone. The image of Wyatt on the phone in Tombstone jars our sense of that time and place. Here's the section he and Flood wrote, mentioning the phone:

"A few minutes before eleven p.m. the United States Deputy Marshal at Tombstone was summoned from his seat in the Grand Hotel by the ringing of the telephone bell.

"Hello!" "Hello!" "Hello!" came the sound of a voice as if it were some distance away. "Is that you, Wyatt?"

"Yes, hello, who is this; I can hardly hear you."

"This is Bob, Bob Paul; can you hear?"

"Oh yes, all right now; where are you?"

"Benson; I just got in." "The coach was attacked, Wyatt; just after we left Drew's ranch." "Bud Philpot and a fellow on the dickey seat were killed and the horses ran away."

"Killed!" "They were!" "Did you get any of the gang?"

"No, they all got away but they left a trail." "I think we have a pretty good chance of nabbing the whole crowd." "Can you come down right away?"

"Yes, right away; I'll get Virg and Morg and Bat." "It'll be thirty minutes before we get started; we'll meet you at the ranch at daylight." "Are you alright yourself?"

But the only reply was a jumble of words, and then he heard the telephone ring off at the other end of the line."

— Flood Manuscript of Wyatt's Autobiography, 1926

"meaning business" and sets off in pursuit. None other than John Clum, mayor of Tombstone, heads this posse. Also in the group are Wyatt Earp; his brother Virgil, newly appointed marshal of Tombstone and voted first lieutenant of this expedition; and Johnny Behan, sheriff of Cochise County and voted captain.

The expedition strikes across Sulphur Springs Valley. Posse member George Parsons reports in his journal: "Hay ranches deserted. At one place, food left [on table]...Horses were half harnessed running about and one or two poor animals were shot by Indians." After leaving the road the posse is struck by a "terrible rain storm."

Soaked and miserable, several posse members slink away and head back for Tombstone. Clum and Parsons fall behind and worry about being "taken in" by the Apaches. Parsons says, "the ground was so soft and soggy, horses going in nearly up to their knees." At ten that night they reach Frink's ranch, where the Apaches had struck earlier in the day.

The posse keeps a close watch on their horses and tries to dry out as they clean their guns and prepare for battle. One man makes some coffee, but another drops his shoe in the coffee pot as he's trying to dry his footwear over the fire. They drink the coffee anyway.

The posse spends a very uncomfortable night. Parsons remembers they "laid all over one another to catch some sleep...I crawled under a table and had to twist legs around one table leg..." When anyone would get up in the night, they flung dirt and water in his face as they splashed around the soggy, earthen bunkhouse floor.

At 3 a.m. the still damp and grumpy posse take off by the light of the moon to find Apaches but they are unsuccessful.

THERE'S NOTHING NEW UNDER THE SUN

IN-LINE SKATES, 1881

LAWN-MOWER, 1879

Adopted by the National League for 1879. Price, mailed, $1 50; Professional Dead, $1 25; Amateur Dead, $1; "Spalding's Base-Ball Guide," 10c.; Catcher's Mask, $3. "Spalding's Journal of American Sports," containing interesting articles on Base Ball, Archery, Lawn Tennis, Croquet, La Crosse, Fishing, and all out-door sports, with prices of the necessary implements, mailed free upon application. Address A. G. SPALDING & BROS., 118 Randolph Street, Chicago, Ill.

SPALDING BASEBALL, 1879

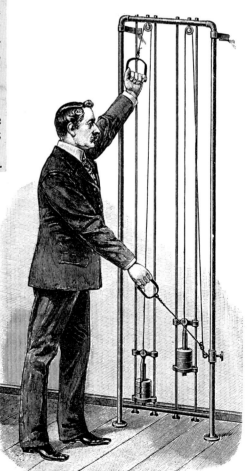

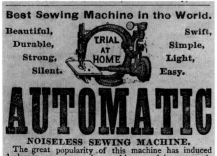

SEWING MACHINE, 1879

MACHINE SHOP, 1881

UNIVERSAL GYM, 1881

HOW TO PLAY DOC'S FAVORITE GAME

THE GAME OF FARO

Faro was the foremost gambling game of the nineteenth century. It was played on a painted oilcloth of thirteen cards of one suit, usually spades. An abacus-like contraption called a "casekeeper" was used to keep a record of the cards that had been played in each deal. A spring-loaded dealer's box held the deck of cards.

Bets were placed by the players on any combination of cards on the layout. The dealer, after shuffling the deck, placed it face up in the box. The top card, the "soda," had no part in the betting. The dealer then drew the cards from a slot in the side of the box in a series of "turns." The first card of a turn was a loser, and won for the banker any wager on that card on the layout; the second was a winner and won for any player who had placed his bet on that particular card. If a "split" appeared, a pair on the turn, the banker took half the wagers on that card. The game was complicated by betting on combinations of cards, parlaying bets, and "coppering" bets, that is betting a card would be a loser rather than a winner. After twenty-four turns there were three cards remaining in the box—a loser, a winner, and the last card, the hock. Players could bet on the order of these last three cards and the bank paid odds, usually four to one, for correct guesses.

Honestly played, faro gave the player a fair chance to win, the dealer's edge being only the money he won from splits. However, a deft card manipulator could, while shuffling, increase the normal incidence of splits by stacking pairs. A number of "gaffed" or crooked faro boxes were introduced by which unscrupulous dealers fleeced players.

—Knights of The Green Cloth by Robert K. DeArment

Turning back, the men retrace their steps across the Sulphur Springs Valley and stop at the McLaury ranch. Here the posse sees "Arizona's most famous outlaw at the present time"—Curly Bill Brocius. Virgil Earp shakes his hand warmly and they "hobnob" for some time. When Curly Bill and his two satellites leave, the posse notices that two pair of spurs are missing.

Also missing is Geronimo and his band, who have escaped into Mexico.

GERONIMO, 1881

October 17, 1881
Morgan Earp is appointed as a Special Police Officer in Tombstone.

October 20, 1881
Ike Clanton corners Earp and demands to know if Wyatt has told Doc about their "agreement." When Earp replies he has not, Clanton is not calmed. Ike grows obsessed with Holliday's possible

knowledge of his intended betrayal of Leonard, Head and Crane. To settle the matter, Wyatt finally sends his brother, Morg, up to Tucson to retrieve Doc Holliday.

October 21, 1881

Doc and Kate are enjoying a sojourn to Tucson for the San Augustin Feast and Fair at Levin Park. It appears the Tucson *Weekly Citizen* knew Doc and Kate were coming because the newspaper wrote on August 25, "As the Feast approaches sharpers of all kinds gather into the city. We must look out for games and tricks of all kinds. Thieves, burglars, pick-pockets and cut throats will be here in large numbers." (The same issue mentions Morgan Earp as a member of Ed Byrne's gang of "top and bottom" thieves at Benson.)

Kate remembers they were there about four days when Morgan came up and tapped Holliday on the shoulder as Doc was "bucking at faro" and said, 'Doc, we want you in Tombstone tomorrow. Better come up this evening."

Doc cashes in his chips. Kate remembers, "Morgan Earp did not want Doc to take me back with them; although he did not say anything."

Doc tries to be firm with Kate, "You had better stay here," he says. "I will come after you tomorrow or in a day or two."

But Kate is adamant—"No, I am going back with you."

Doc tries again: "We are going back on a freight train."

Kate hangs tough—"If you can go on a freight, so can I."

Doc ups the ante: "We are going back on a freight. Then we have to ride on an open buckboard."

"So can I."

The boys give in and Kate wins this pot, adding proudly, "They saw that there was no way of getting rid of me, so the three of us went back to Tombstone (the *Epitaph* reports the two men's return but not Kate's—see opposite page).

LEVIN'S PARK WHERE DOC GAMBLED
Levin's park in Tucson is a popular spot for band concerts, picnics and sporting events. It is here, during the San Augustin Feast, that Morgan Earp walks up and taps Holliday on the shoulder while the doctor is "bucking the tiger." (ARIZONA HISTORICAL SOCIETY)

"If you can go on a freight, so can I."
—KATE

THE BOYS ARE BACK IN TOWN

With Ike Clanton becoming increasingly fearful that Wyatt has told Doc of their deal to get Leonard, Head and Crane, Wyatt sends Morgan Earp to Tucson to bring Doc back. This is interesting because Virgil is already in Tucson for the Stillwell-Spence hearing on the Bisbee stage robbery. The trio; Morg, Doc and Kate, hop a freight and then a buckboard from Benson back to Tombstone. When they arrive, Wyatt is waiting with Ike and simply asks Doc if he knows of any deal between Clanton and himself. When Doc answers in the negative, Wyatt considers the matter closed.

At the left is the newspaper announcement telling of Doc's return on Saturday, October 22, 1881. Ike Clanton leaves town but returns on October 25. Note also the paper's mention of the testing of water hydrants. The recent installation of a water line down the south side of Fremont Street will play a significant part in the events that follow.

Doc, Morgan and Kate ride back to Benson on a freight train in a stock car like the one shown here.

On the evening of October 25, Ike Clanton plays cards with Virgil Earp, Johnny Behan and others in an all-night poker game in the Occidental. When the game breaks up at dawn, Ike reportedly is incensed that Virgil had a pistol in his lap during the game.

PUNCH, OR THE LONDON CHARIVARI.—OCTOBER 22, 1881.

"COLLARED!!"

"I BEG THAT YOU WILL LOOK UPON ME SIMPLY AS REPRESENTING THE EXECUTIVE POWER, AND THE AUTHORITY OF THE LAW."—*The* PREMIER'S *Speech at the Guildhall, Thursday, October* 13.

MERRY OLD IKE!

Armed desperados are not just the concern of the Tombstone Police Department. The above editorial cartoon is from England's Punch magazine. Note the date at top—October 22, 1881.

"As soon as the Earps and Holliday appear the ball will open!"
—IKE CLANTON

COCK-A-DOODLE-CLANTON!
As the sun peeks over Allen Street, Ike Clanton struts up and down crowing to the few who are up and about. Three miners cross the road behind him, on their way to the Vizina Hoisting Works.

October 25, 1881

Ike Clanton and Tom McLaury ride into Tombstone in a spring wagon. They arrive around 11 in the morning and put up at the Grand Hotel. The two of them take in the town trying hard not to miss any of the 66 saloons that saturate the city limits.

Around midnight Ike goes into the Alhambra for a bite to eat. While he's eating, Doc Holliday comes in and starts to call him every name in the book. Ike tries to calm Holliday down, but Doc is drunk and keeps trying to provoke Ike into fighting. The gist of Holliday's anger is that he's disgusted with Ike for 1) even thinking that Doc would betray Wyatt's confidence, and 2) that Ike would even think of betraying his friends. Ike can't win.

Morgan finally intercedes and the two step outside where they go at it again. Virgil Earp comes up and threatens to arrest them both if they don't stop. Doc finally leaves and later, Ike approaches Wyatt as he is closing his faro game at the Eagle Brewery. Clanton tells Wyatt that in the morning he will have "man for man." Wyatt says he doesn't want to fight because "there's no money in it." But Ike continues his feuding harangue until Wyatt tires of the whiskey talk and dismisses Clanton with, "Go home Ike, you talk too much for a fighting man."

Wyatt collects his money and puts it in the safe. On his way home he meets Doc and they walk together up Fourth and west on Fremont to Fly's where Doc is staying with Kate. Wyatt continues on to his home at Third and Fremont.

Ike continues drinking and ends up in an all-night poker game in the Occidental. By morning, he is primed. He retrieves his Winchester and a pistol from the Grand and begins walking the streets yelling at anyone who will listen, "the ball is about to open."

MAN ABOUT TOWN

After the all-night poker game, and before the gunfight, Ike made quite a few stops in between. *(See corresponding numbers in the map, right.)*

1. Near sunrise, Ike leaves the all-night poker game at the Occidental.
2. Ike roams up and down Allen Street yelling threats against the Earps and Holliday *(see illustration previous page).*
3. Ned Boyle sees Ike at 8 a.m. at the telegraph office.
4. Ike retires to Kelly's Wine House, where he continues drinking and grousing to anyone who will listen.
5. Just after noon Ike ambles over to Hafford's Saloon and makes more threats.
6. Ike goes down to Fly's looking for Doc.
7. Ike stands in front of the post office and runs into John Clum.
8. Virgil buffaloes Ike in the alley between Fremont and Allen on Fourth.
9. Virgil hauls Ike to court.
10. Ike goes to Doctor Gillingham's office in the Post Office building.
11. Bandaged and nauseated, Ike goes into Spangenberg's gun shop and tries to buy another gun.
12. Ike walks by the Earps at Hafford's corner and goes back into the Occidental.
13. Ike goes to the Dexter corral and meets his brother and the McLaurys.
14. Ike and the cow-boys cross Allen, going through the O.K. Corral and onto Fremont and the gunfight site.
15. Ike runs and hides in A.H. Emanuel's building.

FOLLOW THE BOUNCING IKE AS HE PING-PONGS AROUND TOMBSTONE

IKE CLANTON

JULIUS "DICK" KELLY

THE BILLIARD PARLOR AT KELLY'S

Saloons in Tombstone were a far cry from the usual movie stereotype. The Nugget *of Oct. 5, 1881 notes "Kelly's has been fitted up...with bowling alley, shooting gallery, bar and cigar store attached." Among drinks dispensed (ad in the* Nugget *of Nov. 23, 1880) were: Pony Whiskey and Brandy, Genuine Irish and Scotch Whiskey, Hot Scotch, Six-year-old Kentucky Apple Brandy, Millers Extra and O.K. Cutter Whiskey, Gin Rum, Sherry, Port, Brandy and Genuine English Ale on Draft. Ike also had his choice of 26 imported wines. One wonders if they ever heard of "Rot-Gut."*

THE DAWN OF THE DYING

"He was dying faster than usual that morning, striping the sides of the dry sink with bloody sputum and shreds of shattered lung. His ears rang and his head felt hollow.

When the first seizure of the day had passed he remained leaning on his palms on the maple washstand, shoulders gathered into a tent behind his lowered head, the stench of evaporated night-sweat stale in his nostrils. On such mornings his senses were painfully acute and he could not stand to be around himself. He poured blood-tinted liquid into a thick, smeared glass tumbler on the stand, set down the bottle, and drank, not lowering the tumbler until it was as empty as his head. The alcohol spread inside him, burning as it went, cauterizing. He replenished the contents of the glass and drank it more slowly. The sharp barley fumes flushed his own stink from his olfactory system."

—Loren D. Estleman, in the opening to his book "Bloody Season" Published by Bantam

"On going out [Doc] said, 'I won't be here to take you to breakfast, so you had better go alone.' I didn't go to breakfast. I don't remember whether I ate anything or not that day."

—KATE

October 26, 1881

Around 8:45 a.m. Ned Boyle wakes Wyatt Earp and tells him of Ike's threats. Boyle quotes Ike as saying, "As soon as those damned Earps make their appearance on the street today, the ball will open. We are looking for the sons of bitches!"

Officer Andy Bronk comes down to Virgil's house (he lives kitty-corner from Wyatt) for commitment papers regarding a prisoner. While Virgil is getting it, Bronk says, "You had better get up. There is liable to be hell. Ike Clanton has threatened to kill Holliday as soon as he gets up. He's counting you fellows in too." Virgil waves Bronk off and goes back to bed, hoping the situation will take care of itself.

Virgil is awakened again and told Ike is hunting him with a Winchester. Virgil gets dressed and goes up town.

Doc sleeps late. Around noon, Kate rousts him out of bed. "Doc, Ike Clanton is looking for you and had a rifle with him."

"If God will let me live long enough," Doc says, "he will see me."

WHISKEY BRAVADO
Ike Clanton has already put a dent in Tombstone's whiskey supply, but Doc Holliday just got up.

HIGH NOON

At noon, Ike Clanton brings his one-man riot to Hafford's Saloon. Brandishing a rifle, Clanton recounts how Holliday and the Earps have insulted him. Last night he was unarmed, but now he is heeled. Doc and the Earps have agreed to meet him before noon, he declares. Checking his pocket watch, Ike grumbles, "It is five minutes past twelve now." Colonel Hafford corrects Clanton, "It is ten minutes past," he says, gesturing toward the saloon clock, "You had better go home. There will be nothing of it." Ignoring the Colonel's wise counsel, Ike Clanton marches out to hunt up Doc Holliday. Instead, Ike meets Virgil south of the post office.

(BBB*)

THE BIRDS
There aren't enough birds to quench Colonel Roderick Ferdinand Hafford's peculiar aesthetic. He gluts his saloon with stuffed fowl. In this photo (below), he stands proudly behind the bar Ike Clanton visits before the famous gunfight. Virgil Earp and Johnny Behan will also meet in Haffords on October 26, 1881 when they discuss strategy. (COURTESY OF TOMBSTONE COURTHOUSE STATE HISTORIC PARK)

TOMBSTONE, 1881

(BBB*)

Virgil Earp comes up behind Ike Clanton in an alley-way on Fourth Street, and says, "I hear you're looking for some of us."

With that he slams the barrel of his revolver against the side of Ike's head. Morgan Earp and Virg then drag Clanton to Judge Wallace's courtroom where, after a heated-hearing, Ike is fined $27.50 for carrying weapons.

When Wyatt Earp leaves the courtroom he bumps into Tom McLaury. The two exchange words and Wyatt slaps Tom and buffaloes him, sending him sprawling into the street.

As Ike Clanton is having his skull tended to by Dr. Gillingham, Frank McLaury and Bill Clanton ride in from Antelope Springs and dismount at the Grand Hotel. Seeing the new arrivals sparks the devil in Doc and he walks right up and shakes Billy Clanton's hand.

Puzzled by Doc's cheery display, Frank and Billy retire to the Grand Hotel bar for a drink. At the bar, Billy Allen asks Frank McLaury if he's heard what's going on. When told of Wyatt Earp's buffaloing of his brother Tom, Frank rises agitated. "What did he hit Tom for?" he asks. Then he declares, "We won't drink." With that, the cow-boys leave the barroom in search of Ike Clanton.

Doc Holliday's movements are hard to trace. After leaving Kate, he evidently headed to a restaurant for breakfast. Then he went to the Alhambra Saloon to see about a game. While there, Morgan Earp came in to advise him of the growing tension between the Earps and the cow-boys. Doc joins the Earps at Hafford's Corner.

The Grand Hotel (above with the gabled roof) *was the designated cow-boy headquarters in Tombstone.*

"Doc Holliday met Billy Clanton...and shook hands with him and told him he was pleased to meet him."
—Ike Clanton

PLEASED TO MEET YOU, HOPE TO KILL YOU SOON!

Certainly one of the most bizarre turns in the byzantine events that lead up to the gunfight, is Doc's handshake with Billy Clanton in front of the Grand Hotel. Given the previous evening's fireworks with older brother Ike, Doc has to be taunting the younger Clanton with ironic humor.

THE WALK DOWN

"Come along," Virgil Earp says as he hands the Wells Fargo shotgun to Doc Holliday. As the quartet starts up Fourth Street, Morgan Earp turns to Wyatt and says, "They have horses, had we not better get some horses ourselves, so that if they make a running fight we can catch them?" "No" Wyatt replies matter of factly, "If they try to make a running fight we can kill their horses then capture them."

At first the men walk four abreast. At Fremont Street they turn left and walk two by two on the south sidewalk.

After twenty minutes of failed persuasion, Johnny Behan hasn't gotten anywhere. Billy Clanton swears he wants to leave town and Frank McLaury won't hear of

G. F. SPANGENBERG,

PIONEER GUNSMITH AND Locksmith.

212 FOURTH STREET, NEAR BROWN'S HOTEL.

DEALER IN GUNS, PISTOLS, CARTRIDGES, CUTLERY, SEWING MACHINES, Etc.

The Only Complete Gun and Locksmithing Shop in Arizona

giving up his pistol unless the Earp party is disarmed. Tom McLaury seems unusually quiet. When they see the Earps and Holliday appear on Fremont Street, the cow-boys all pull back deeper into the lot.

Since Doc has no experience as an officer, Morgan briefs him on tactic and procedure. It would be best to let Virgil do the talking. Doc should post himself on the street to cover their right flank. Morgan says if anyone moves, "This time let them have it." Some onlookers think Doc is whistling under his mustaches. Knowing Holliday's temper, he is probably seething as well. The cow-boys are *at his house!* His woman is inside and armed men who have already

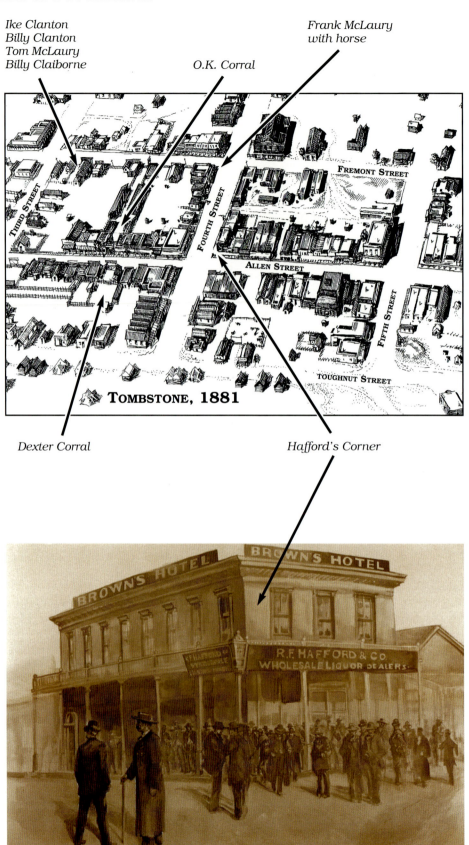

Ike Clanton
Billy Clanton
Tom McLaury
Billy Claiborne

O.K. Corral

Frank McLaury
with horse

TOMBSTONE, 1881

Dexter Corral

Hafford's Corner

CROWD PLEASERS

As the afternoon wears on, quite a crowd gathers at Hafford's corner expecting a fight. While Wyatt and Virgil talk to various townsmen, Morgan and Doc (above left) stand in the center of Allen and Fourth streets and look for signs of the cow-boys.

*"That's a hell of a thing
for you to say to me."*
—DOC HOLLIDAY, RESPONDING TO WYATT'S
COMMENT, "THIS ISN'T YOUR FIGHT, DOC."

SHOOTING THE BREEZE
(l to r) Billy Claiborne talks to Billy Clanton as Tom
McLaury leans out of the lot and looks up Fremont; Ike
Clanton looks dazed and Frank McLaury refuses to give
up his arms to Johnny Behan unless the Earps and
Holliday are disarmed. Billy Clanton has tied his horse to
a post next to the Harwood house.

FIVE COW-BOYS IN A ROW
(l to r) Billy Claiborne, Billy Clanton, Tom McLaury, Ike Clanton, Frank McLaury and Frank's horse. Note: Tom McLaury's untucked shirt and the liquor bottles.

been to his residence once before and threatened his life, are outside Kate's window. This fact must have brought Doc's blood up, to say the least. This dynamic of the fight has never been sufficiently explored: If any man came home and saw armed men in his yard, who wouldn't fight to protect his loved ones?!

Meanwhile, seeing the Earps and Holliday approach, Behan tells the cow-boys to wait while he goes up to stop the marshal and his men. Hurrying up the street he meets the city marshal under the striped awning of the Union Market. Johnny holds up his hands and shouts, "Hold up boys, don't go down there or there will be trouble!" Virgil is firm. "Johnny, I am going down to disarm them!"

"I have been down there to disarm them!" Behan cries. But the Earps and Holliday never break stride.

Wes Fuller arrives breathlessly to warn of the Earps' dire intentions. But he is too late.

"Hold up boys, don't go down there or there will be trouble; I have been down there to disarm them!"
—SHERIFF JOHN BEHAN

After Behan implies he disarmed the cow-boys, the marshal and his men push ahead. Virgil puts his pistol in his waistband—far back on the left hip. Wyatt slips his shooter into his coat pocket.

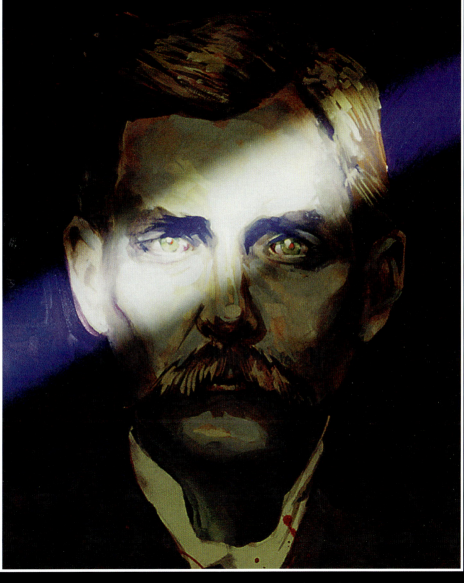

"The son-of-a-bitch has shot me, and I mean to kill him."

GUNSMOKE

Of all the guns of the frontier, none would be more precious than those used at the O.K. Corral shootout. Should a shotgun show up that could be verified as the weapon Doc Holliday used on October 26, 1881, it would fetch at least six figures. Court records definitely identify Frank McLaury's and Billy Clanton's pistols as Colt .44-.40 Frontier Six-Shooters. Frank McLaury's revolver, serial number 46338, was shipped to J.P. Moore's Sons, New York City on September 27, 1878. Billy Clanton's shooter, serial number 52196, was shipped to Simmon's Hardware Company, St. Louis, Missouri, on July 19, 1879. Either of these weapons would bring a fortune today.

None of the guns the Earps and Doc Holliday used that day were carefully identified by serial number at the time. The *Nugget* of October 27, 1881 tells us "...Doc Holliday shot Tom McLaury in the right side, using a short shotgun, such as is carried by Wells Fargo & Co. messengers." Generally it is believed this was a 10-gauge shotgun, but specific confirmation of this has not surfaced. All we know about Doc Holliday's pistol is that it was nickel-plated. The caliber and make of Doc's revolver are a matter of conjecture. The Earp guns are equally shrouded in mystery.

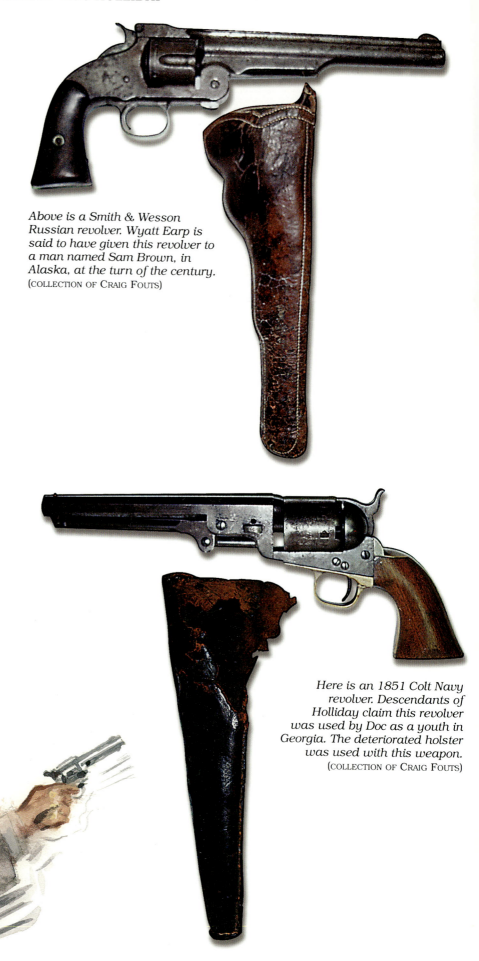

Above is a Smith & Wesson Russian revolver. Wyatt Earp is said to have given this revolver to a man named Sam Brown, in Alaska, at the turn of the century.
(COLLECTION OF CRAIG FOUTS)

Here is an 1851 Colt Navy revolver. Descendants of Holliday claim this revolver was used by Doc as a youth in Georgia. The deteriorated holster was used with this weapon.
(COLLECTION OF CRAIG FOUTS)

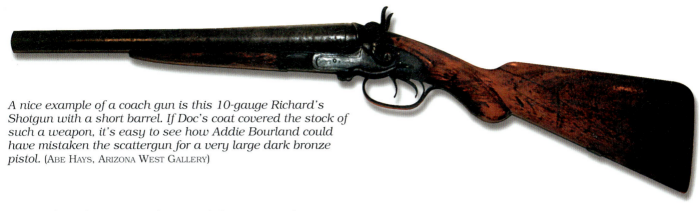

A nice example of a coach gun is this 10-gauge Richard's Shotgun with a short barrel. If Doc's coat covered the stock of such a weapon, it's easy to see how Addie Bourland could have mistaken the scattergun for a very large dark bronze pistol. (ABE HAYS, ARIZONA WEST GALLERY)

"Only the good Lord knows how many have shelled out to buy Doc Holliday's shotgun or Wyatt Earp's Buntline Special."
—ALFORD E. TURNER,
AUTHOR WRITING IN "INQUEST"

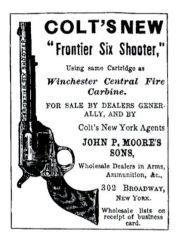

COLT'S NEW
"Frontier Six Shooter,"
Using same Cartridge as
Winchester Central Fire Carbine.
FOR SALE BY DEALERS GENER-
ALLY, AND BY
Colt's New York Agents
JOHN P. MOORE'S SONS,
Wholesale Dealers in Arms,
Ammunition, &c.,
302 BROADWAY,
NEW YORK.
Wholesale lists on
receipt of business
card.

This derringer was allegedly given to Doc Holliday by Big Nose Kate. It's a .41 caliber Remington Double Derringer with the serial number 474, which tells us it was manufactured in the 1870s.

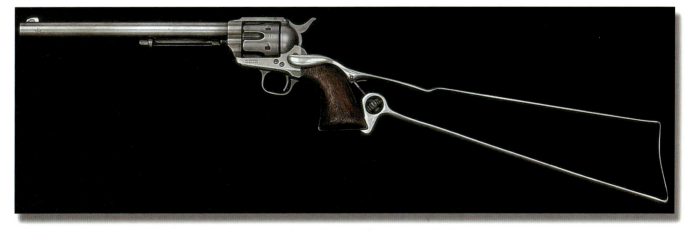

This long-barreled Colt .45, serial #28830, was shipped to Tombstone gun dealer S. L. Hart on May 12, 1882. A special-order item, this pistol was probably ordered while the Earps and Doc were still in town. Its 10-inch barrel makes it a most intriguing weapon as Stuart Lake's interview notes with Wyatt Earp claim Wyatt's special revolver had a 10-inch barrel. By the time Lake's book "Frontier Marshal" appeared in print, however, he was claiming Earp's gun had a 12-inch barrel.

WHY DID IT BECOME KNOWN AS "GUNFIGHT AT THE O.K. CORRAL"?

The "Gunfight in the Vacant Lot—Next to Fly's—Down the Block From The Rear Entrance to the O.K. Corral." Nope, won't work. It wouldn't fit on a theater marquee. Frankie Lane would never sing the song.

By now it's a well-known misnomer, but how did it come about? On October 27, 1881 the *Nugget* wrote: "...at this time Sheriff Behan appeared upon the scene and told Marshal Earp...he would go down to the O.K. Corral, where Ike and Billy Clanton and Frank and Tom McLaury were and disarm them..." Later, in this same report we're told "...as he [Virgil] and his posse came down Fremont Street towards the corral, the sheriff stepped out..." So it was that one of the earliest reports of the shooting placed the affray at the O.K. Corral.

In a 1907 article, Bat Masterson placed the shooting near the corral gate. Frederick Brechdolt repeated that placement in his 1919 article, "Tombstone's Wild Oats." In 1928 both Lorenzo Walters ("Tombstone's Yesterday") and Billy Breckenridge ("Helldorado") identified photos of the corral as the shooting site. Finally in 1926, Wyatt Earp, himself, drew maps *(see right)* pinpointing the corral as the site.

Following these leads, Stuart Lake headlined his chapter of the shooting—"At the O.K. Corral" ("Frontier Marshal," 1931).

From there the title caught on and the rest is semi-history.

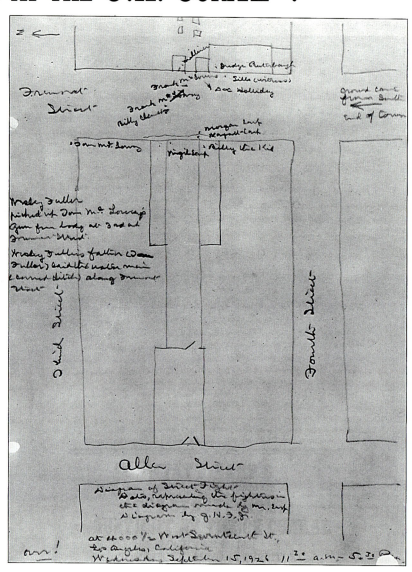

WYATT'S HAND-DRAWN MAP OF THE GUNFIGHT
In 1926 Wyatt Earp produced a map of the gunfight site. The problem with the map is that it locates the shootout at the rear entrance of the O.K. Corral. That Wyatt would misremember the location of such an important event seems incredible, but it had been forty-five years. This document is on display at the Gene Autry Museum in Los Angeles.

WYATT EARP, 1928

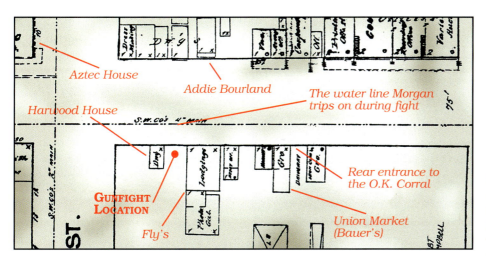

Aztec House

Addie Bourland

Harwood House

The water line Morgan trips on during fight

Rear entrance to the O.K. Corral

GUNFIGHT LOCATION

Fly's

Union Market (Bauer's)

ST.

The Sanborn map (above) was executed in the summer of 1882. It clearly shows a small house west of Fly's. This appears to be at odds with the photo below.

THE EARLIEST KNOWN PHOTO OF THE GUNFIGHT SITE...

Looking east from Comstock Hill, the 1881 photo *(below)* clearly shows the roof of the Aztec House beyond which appears Fly's Lodging House and Photo Gallery. There, before our eyes, is the most famous vacant lot in frontier history with the two smaller buildings lying to the west.

According to the maps of the period, the lot measured about eighteen feet in width at the time of the shooting. Most news reports, however, stated the width as fifteen feet.

What's curious about the blowup of the photo *(see left)*, is that the Harwood house and the house to the west of it, appear to have twin long roofs. But the Sanborn map of 1882 shows the Harwood house to be small (in the Sanborn map, the corner house is gone). This matches testimony of four of the witnesses at the Spicer Hearing who specifically described it as a "little house."

Fly's Lodging

Harwood House Location

Aztec House

GUNFIGHT LOCATION

Corner House

VIRGIL'S HOUSE

TOMBSTONE, LOOKING EAST FROM COMSTOCK HILL, 1881 (ARIZONA HISTORICAL SOCIETY)

THE MOMENT OF TRUTH-A MISDEMEANOR ARREST GONE AWRY

When the Earps and Holliday enter the narrow space between Fly's and the Harwood house they confront quite a crowd. In addition to Ike and Billy Clanton, Tom and Frank McLaury, there is Billy Claiborne (who is fading fast), Johnny Behan and Wes Fuller, who has come to warn Billy Clanton of the Earp's bloody intent. Unfortunately for Billy, Wes got sidetracked from his mission by Mattie Webb, a saloon owner and prostitute.

*"Frank McLaury had
hold of a horse,
about the corner of a post."*
—BILLY CLAIBORNE

WHERE DID SHERIFF BEHAN GO?

SHERIFF JOHN BEHAN

From the moment Behan confronted the Earps near the Union Market (Bauer's) to the opening shots of the gunfight, the sheriff's movements are a mystery. Did he follow the Earps into the lot? Or, did he make his way through the lodging house as some speculate? We don't know because he never tells us. The next place Behan shows up is on the landing between the lodging house and the gallery. Billy Claiborne has retreated towards the landing and he testifies that during the gunfight, Behan grabbed him and pulled him to safety in the gallery.

THE DEADLY DUO

Many of the eyewitnesses believed Doc Holliday *(with shotgun)* and Morgan Earp started the fight. When the Earp party passed Bauer's, Martha King overheard Morgan say, "Let them have it." She later testified that Holliday replied, "All right." A chorus of cow-boy witnesses pinned the fight squarely on Holliday as the most discreditable member in the Earp party.

In 1976 an alleged memoir of Josephine Earp gave widespread credence to the story. However, in recent years doubts have arisen over the authenticity of that section of those recollections.

*"I had my pistol in my overcoat pocket,
where I had put it when Behan had
told us he had disarmed the other parties.
When I saw Billy Clanton and
Frank McLaury draw their pistols,
I drew my pistol."*
—WYATT EARP

Wyatt (above) stands to the right, slightly behind his brother Virgil, and remains at the northwest corner of Fly's lodging house for most of the fight. Behind him we can see Kate peering through the lodging house window. She relates, "This lady friend (Mrs. Fly) and I went to the side window, which faced the vacant lot. One shot went through the window, just two panes above us. My friend left the window, but I stayed there until the fight was over."

HOW OLD WERE THE GUNFIGHTERS?

DOC HOLLIDAY, 30

WYATT EARP, 33

VIRGIL EARP, 38

MORGAN EARP, 30

FRANK McLAURY, 33
TOM McLAURY, 28
BILLY CLANTON, 19
IKE CLANTON, 34

"HOLD ON, I DON'T WANT THAT!"

As the ranking officer, Virgil Earp boldly walks into the vacant lot. "Boys, throw up your hands," he demands, "I want your guns."

Frank McLaury says, "We will," but at the same time makes a motion to pull his revolver.

Doc Holliday crowds Tom McLaury and thrusts the shotgun in his gut.

Morgan Earp stands on the sidewalk looking straight into the lot. Ike Clanton blocks Morgan's view of Billy.

Viewing Frank as the most

VIRGIL EARP TRIES TO PREVENT THE FIGHT

dangerous, Wyatt isn't taking any chances. He jerks his shooter from his coat pocket.

Blind to Frank's move, Billy sees Earp's draw as unprovoked. He swiftly pulls his own revolver and aims at Wyatt.

With the situation slipping from control, Virgil exhorts, "Hold on, I don't want that!"

Two shots reverberate nearly as one; Billy's shot goes wide, passing between Wyatt and Morgan.

Wyatt Earp's lead ball slams into Frank McLaury's belly.

Billy Clanton   Ike Clanton   Frank McLaury   Tom McLaury   Doc Holliday

Wes Fuller   Billy Claiborne   Johnny Behan   Virgil Earp   Wyatt Earp   Morgan Earp

THIS FIGHT'S COMMENCED!

After the first two shots there is a pause. All of the participants are stunned by the abruptness of the shooting. Suddenly sober, Ike runs up and grapples with Wyatt. This prevents Billy from getting another clear shot at Earp. Ike's movement now allows Morgan a clear shot at Billy which he quickly acts on, hitting the young cow-boy in the chest. A gutshot Frank McLaury, seen staggering towards the street, fires and hits Virgil in the right calf. Tom McLaury, behind the second horse, takes aim at Morgan and will hit the youngest Earp across the shoulders. The

SHERIFF BEHAN (left) **"FIRES" BILLY CLAIBORNE INTO THE PHOTO GALLERY AS BILLY CLANTON** (extreme right) **GOES TO FIGHTING**

bullet enters the right shoulder, rips across his back and punches out the left shoulder. (The lead ball was found in Morgan's shirtsleeve.) As Wyatt and Ike continue to struggle, Earp's gun discharges into the ground. Clanton begs for his life as Earp pushes him off roaring, "This fight has commenced. Get to fighting or get out!" Clanton chooses the latter and flees around the corner of Fly's into the boarding house, out the back door, through the photo gallery and across Allen Street to safety. As he runs he hears a bullet whiz past his head.

(l to r) *Billy Clanton, Virgil Earp, Ike Clanton, Wyatt Earp, Tom McLaury* (behind second horse), *Morgan Earp and Frank McLaury. Doc Holliday is obscured by smoke while trying to get a clear shot at Tom.*

DID TOM MCLAURY HAVE A WEAPON?

Wyatt Earp always believed that Tom McLaury had a pistol and that it was he who wounded Morgan. However, no weapon was found either on McLaury's body or on the scene (in later years, Wyatt claimed Wes Fuller picked up the gun).

"If Tom McLaury was unarmed, I did not know it. I believe he was armed and fired two shots at our party before Holliday, who had the shotgun, fired and killed him."
—Wyatt Earp

"Tom McLaury might have had a pistol and I not know of it."
—John Behan

"I never saw him [Tom] with any arms during the shooting."
—Ike Clanton

"Tom McLaury threw open his coat and said, 'I haven't got anything, boys, I am disarmed.' Then the shooting commenced..."
—Billy Claiborne

If Tom McLaury did shoot Morgan, the movement of Frank McLaury out of the lot is easy to explain. While Wyatt is tending to his downed brother Morgan, and Doc is preoccupied with Tom—a window of opportunity opens for Frank to move past his adversaries. However, if Tom didn't shoot Morg, Frank's advance past Doc becomes a puzzle.

If Tom was unarmed, then only Billy Clanton could have shot Morgan. Some believe that Billy hit the younger Earp across the shoulders when Morgan turned to fire at Ike Clanton as he ran into the front of Fly's. Both the *Epitaph* and the *Nugget* claim Billy's shot did the damage. The debate goes on.

"At the crack of the first two pistols, the horse jumped to one side, and Tom McLaury failed to get the Winchester. He threw his hand back this way [shows the motion]. He followed the movement of the horse around, making him a kind of breastwork, and fired once, if not twice, over the horse's back." —Virgil Earp

"A horse makes a good breastwork, but a bad gunrest."
—ALFRED HENRY LEWIS,
IN "SUNSET TRAIL" 1905

"I'M HIT!" *Morgan says as he goes down.*

THE DOCTOR WILL SEE YOU NOW

As Wyatt Earp shoots at the withers of Billy Clanton's horse, Tom McLaury becomes exposed to Doc's line of fire. Holliday doesn't hesitate and pumps 12 buckshot into Tom McLaury's right side.

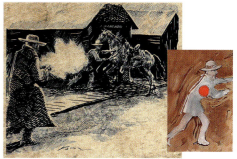

The mortal wound catches Tom under the right armpit, tearing away the flesh from his triceps. The positioning of the wound shows that McLaury was facing out away from the lot, towards the street. He was either in the act of turning to flee, or trying to maintain his horse as a shield. The cow-boys claimed that Tom was in the act of surrendering when he was shot down. However, if Tom was raising his hands, submitting to Virgil Earp's command, it would have been virtually impossible to have been shot in the right side as he was.

After the shotgun blast hits Tom McLaury, he takes off running like a deer. Holliday, thinking he has missed, throws the scattergun down in disgust. Tom will collapse at the telegraph pole on the corner of Third and Fremont.

WHO SHOT WHO?

By most accounts there were about thirty shots fired during the gunfight. They were fired by:

Frank McLaury—fired four times. His first shot hit Virgil in the right calf. His second was at Wyatt, hitting his coat. The third was at Morgan, but Frank was weak by then and his shot went harmlessly into the ground; his fourth shot was at Holliday, grazing Doc's right hip.

Billy Clanton—fired six times and hit no one.

Tom Mclaury—fired two or three times (assuming he had a weapon), hitting Morgan across the shoulders.

Wyatt Earp—probably fired five shots. His first shot hit Frank McLaury in the belly. His second went into the ground while wrestling with Ike. His third shot was at Frank McLaury and his fourth was at Billy Clanton. Finally, his fifth was fired towards the gallery behind Fly's as Wyatt returned fire he believed was coming from the landing between the buildings (most likely a door slamming—as Ike ran from the area—which Wyatt mistakenly thought was a weapon discharging).

Morgan Earp—probably fired five times. His first shot hit Billy Clanton in the chest. His next three shots were also at Billy Clanton and one of them hit Billy in the right wrist. His fifth shot hit Frank McLaury under the right ear.

Virgil Earp—fired four times. His first shot at Frank McLaury was a miss. And three shots were fired at Billy Clanton, one of which hit Billy in the stomach.

Doc Holliday—His first blast from the shotgun hit Tom McLaury in the right side. Throwing the shotgun down, Doc jerked his handgun and fired two quick shots at Billy Clanton and missed. He finally confronted Frank McLaury in the middle of the street and fired. Conflicting reports indicate that Doc may, or may not, have hit Frank in the chest.

> *"At the same time there was a tall man with gray clothes and broad hat standing about the middle of the street, [who] fired two [shots] apparently in the direction of the man leaning against the house."*
>
> —C. H. LIGHT
> DESCRIBING DOC HOLLIDAY
> SHOOTING AT BILLY CLANTON DURING THE GUNFIGHT

"...the marshal changed the cane from one hand to the other and pulled his revolver out. He seemed to be hit at that time and fell down. He got up immediately and went to shooting."

—H.F. SILLS, TRAIN ENGINEER AND EYEWITNESS

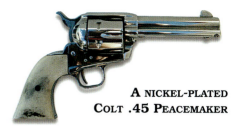

A NICKEL-PLATED COLT .45 PEACEMAKER

A BLUED COLT .45 PEACEMAKER

DOC THE JUGGLER?

Everyone now knows that Doc Holliday carried a shotgun and used it in the fight. Incredible as it seems, many of the witnesses who testified at the Spicer hearing, could not positively identify or even distinguish the use of a shotgun in the fight. Perhaps because all the cow-boy witnesses were bent on pinning the fight squarely on Holliday, there is a preponderance of testimony about the "nickel-plated" pistol, totally ignoring the shotgun. This is probably because everybody in Tombstone knew Doc carried a nickel-plated pistol. From this confusion in the testimony there has evolved a gaggle of theories as to which weapon Doc used first, and how. One wild theory even has Doc using the shotgun in one hand and the pistol in the other and switching back and forth like a frontier juggler.

However, after all the "nickel-plated" finger-pointing on the stand, Doc's lawyer asks a telling question: "Is it not a fact that the first shot fired by Holliday was from a shotgun; that he then threw the shotgun down and drew the nickel-plated pistol from his person and then discharged the nickel-plated pistol?" In later years, Kate would confirm this scenario in her recollections.

"Mr. [Virgil] Earp says that it was the first shot from Frank McLaury that hit him."

—TOMBSTONE *EPITAPH*, OCTOBER 27, 1881

"It is foolish that a cow rustler gunman can come up to a city gunman in a gunfight."
—BIG NOSE KATE

OUTWARD BOUND

From the first shots fired to the end of the fight, the movement of the cow-boys indicates flight.

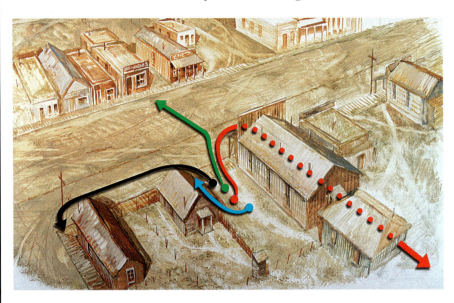

- **The path of Tom McLaury**
- **The path of Frank McLaury**
- **The path of Billy Clanton**
- **The path of Ike Clanton**

BILLY CLANTON—GAME TO THE END

BILLY'S WRIST WOUND

Judge Spicer wrote, "William Clanton was wounded on the wrist of the right hand on the first fire and thereafter used his pistol with his left." However, no evidence was ever presented which proved the "first fire" hit Billy's wrist. Thomas Keefe examined Billy's wound and said, "It went from the inside to the outside." The ball entered Billy's forearm about two inches below the base of the thumb and exited diagonally out the back of the arm in line with the middle finger.

If Billy Clanton was shooting a revolver when this wound was inflicted, it would have probably happened after he went down. The downward trajectory is hard to explain otherwise.

However, Spicer was clearly wrong when he said, "This wound is such as could not have been received with his hands thrown up..." Obviously, Billy could clearly have been hit this way with his hands raised.

"When they got to the corner of Fly's building, they had their six-shooters in their hands, and Marshal Earp said, 'You sons-of-bitches, you've been looking for a fight, and you can have it!' And then he said, 'Throw up your hands.'"
—BILLY CLAIBORNE

GOOD COP, BAD COP

When Virgil Earp allowed Doc Holliday to accompany the arresting party, the town marshal was using poor judgment as a police officer—*versus*—when Virgil allowed Doc to join them in a confrontation with desperate men, the oldest Earp was using excellent judgment, because of Holliday's deadly reputation.

"...I have always felt that his [Virgil's] selection [of Doc Holliday] on that occasion was a very unfortunate one."
—JOHN P. CLUM, MAYOR OF TOMBSTONE

LETTING BILLY HAVE IT
Virgil (with cane), Wyatt and Doc all unload at Billy Clanton. One newspaper claimed the Harwood house behind Billy had nine bullet holes in it.

Of all the witnesses to testify, Virgil was the only shooter who told how many times he fired and who he shot at: "I fired four shots. One at Frank McLaury, and I believe the other three were at Billy Clanton."

THE ARRESTING FIGHTERS

The heart of the controversy over the Earps' actions on October 26, 1881 centers on whether they were lawmen doing their duty, or whether they were gunmen looking for a fight. Judging from the above quote by Billy Claiborne, it appears the Earps were also confused about the difference. An officer of the law doesn't dare hostile men to fight it out and "throw up your hands" at the same time. Whether Virgil Earp actually said both comments is irrelevant. The fact is the Earps and Holliday were sending out a very conflicting message—we're lawmen, but this afternoon we're here specifically to kick your butt.

You're a Daisy if You Do

Of all the shots fired, the final confrontation between Frank McLaury and Doc Holliday was most clearly commented on by eyewitnesses. Bob Hatch: "Saw Doc Holliday and...Frank McLaury near the middle of Fremont Street, probably about ten or twelve feet apart. McLaury made a remark like this: 'I've got you this time!' McLaury seemed to be retreating across the street...as he got near the corner of an adobe building...he stopped and stood with a pistol across his arm, in the act of shooting..."

The *Nugget* also described the scene: "As he [Frank McLaury] started across the street, however, he pulled his gun down on Holliday saying, 'I've got you now.' 'Blaze away! You're a daisy if you have,' replied Doc."

In 1896, Wyatt Earp recalled, "Morgan wheeled around and in doing so fell on his side. While in that position he caught sight of Doc Holliday and Frank McLaury aiming at each other. With a quick drop he shot McLaury in the head. At the same instant, McLaury's pistol flashed and Doc Holliday was shot in the hip."

Billy Clanton is still shooting. That boy will not stay dead. Finally, he feebly fires a last shot up into the air and the gunfight is over.

A throng of people rush up. As bystanders crowd in, they notice that, incredibly, Frank's lips are still moving. Doc tries to make his way through the thickening mob. He bellows, "The son-of-a-bitch has shot me and I mean to kill him!"

Recently filled water line

In 1896, 1920 and again in 1926, Wyatt Earp claimed his brother Morgan went down twice in the gunfight. The second fall was a trip over the recently installed water line on Fremont Street. When Wyatt thought they were under fire from the back of Fly's he called out a warning to Morg. His younger brother turned sharply and tripped over the uneven ground.

"Doc Holliday was as calm as if at target practice and fired rapidly."
—R.F. COLEMAN

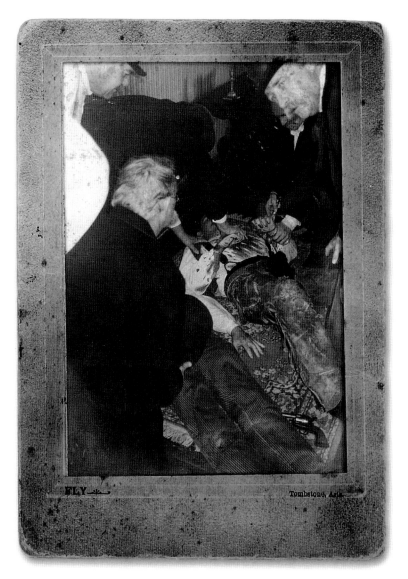

While Tom McLaury stiffens on the carpet, Billy Clanton thrashes about. Thomas Keefe said "Billy was shot through the right wrist, his arm was broken; he was shot on the left side of the belly; he was shot below the left nipple and the lung was oozing blood out of the wound." (PHOTO BY BBB*)

"After the fight was over, Doc came in, and sat on the side of the bed and cried and said, 'Oh, this is just awful—awful.'"
—BIG NOSE KATE

"THEY HAVE MURDERED ME!"

Bracing his left arm across his right knee, Billy Clanton's last shot goes wild into the air. Vainly he tries to fire again but is out of ammo. Both Wyatt's and Morgan's weapons are empty. Virgil has one round left and Doc's pistol holds two bullets, but no one wants to shoot that boy again. Bob Hatch runs to the lot from Bauer's just as C.S. Fly appears with a rifle. "Take that pistol away from him," Fly yells, "or I will kill him."

"Go and get it yourself, if you want it," Hatch replies. As Billy begs for more cartridges, Fly yanks the boy's shooter from his grasp. Tom McLaury and Billy Clanton are carried into the house on the S.E. corner of Third and Fremont.

When Johnny Behan approaches, Wyatt Earp looks down on a fallen cow-boy and says, "We won't have to disarm that party." Behan tries to arrest Earp, but S.B. Comstock interjects, "There is no hurry in arresting this man. He done just right in killing them, and the people will uphold them."

Now indoors and lying next to Tom McLaury, Billy Clanton thrashes about in agony and is given massive doses of morphine. "They have murdered me!..." he screams. The Earp's wounds are treated at a nearby drugstore. They are put in a buggy and taken home. Among some the mood is jubilant—another reason for a good stiff drink. Three blocks away, in Judge Lucas' old office on Toughnut Street, Ike Clanton is found bug-eyed and all a-tremble. With a bad hangover, a sore noggin, two friends dead, a kid brother dying and now on his way to jail, Ike Clanton's day has once again failed to live up to his high expectations.

YESTERDAY'S TRAGEDY

Three Men Hurled into Eternity in the Duration of a Moment.

Stormy as were the early days of Tombstone, nothing ever occurred equal to the event of yesterday. Since the retirement of Ben Sippy as marshal and the appointment of V. W. Earp to fill the vacancy, the town has been noted for its quietness and good order. The fractious and formerly much dreaded cow-boys when they, came to town were upon their good behavior, and no unseemly brawls were indulged in, and it was hoped by our citizens that no more such deeds would occur as led to the killing of Marshal White, one year ago. It seems that this quiet state of affairs was but the calm that precedes the storm that burst in all its fury yesterday, with this difference in results, that the lightning's bolt struck in a different quarter than the one that fell one year ago. This time it struck with its full and awful force upon those who, heretofore, have made the good name of this country a byword and a reproach, instead of upon some officer in the discharge of his duty or a peaceable and unoffending citizen.

Some time Tuesday Ike Clanton came into town, and during the evening had some little talk with Doc Holliday and Marshal Earp, but nothing that caused either to suspect, further than their general knowledge of the man and the threats that had previously been conveyed to the Marshal that the gang intended to clean out the Earps, that he was thirsting for blood at this time, with one exception, and that was that Clanton had told the Marshal, in answer to a question, that the McLowrys were in Sonora. Shortly after this occurred some one came to the Marshal and told him the McLowrys had been seen a short time before, just below town. Marshal Earp, not knowing what might happen and feeling his responsibility for the preservation of the peace and order of the city, staid on duty all night and added to the police force his brother Morgan and Holliday. The night passed without any disturbance whatever, and at sunrise he went home and retired to rest and sleep. A short time afterward one of his brothers came to his house and told him that Clanton was hunting him, with threats of shooting him on sight. He discredited the report and did not get out of bed. It was not long before another of his broth-

THE COW-BOY ORGAN PIPES OFF

Both of Tombstone's newspapers, The *Epitaph* (see their florid lead article at left) and The *Nugget* ran extensive coverage of the fight.

In light of later testimony by Johnny Behan, it is interesting to ponder The *Nugget's* treatment of the shooting on the morning after the gunfight. The reporting for this account was done immediately after the fight before the lawyers became involved. Since the editor, Harry Woods, is also Behan's undersheriff, it seems probable that the following narrative was drawn primarily from Johnny Behan himself. Keep in mind that both men are pro-cow-boy. Here is a section on the gunfight as it appeared in The *Nugget* on Thursday, October 27, 1881. All misspellings and typos have been left as is:

...as [Virgil's] posse came down Fremont Street towards the corral, the Sheriff stepped out and said: "Hold up boys, don't go down there or there will be trouble; I have been down there to disarm them." But they passed on, and when within a few feet of them the Marshal said to the Clantons and McLowrys: "Throw up your hands boys, I intend to disarm you."
As he spoke Frank McLowry made a motion to draw his revolver, when Wyatt Earp pulled his and shot him, the ball striking on the right side of the abdomen. About the same time Doc Holliday shot Tom McLowry in the right side, using a short shotgun, such as is carried by Wells-Fargo & Co.'s messengers. In the meantime Billy Clanton had shot at Morgan Earp, the ball passing through the left shoulder blade across his back, just grazing the backbone and coming out the shoulder, the ball remaining inside of his shirt. He fell to the ground but in an instant gathered himself and raising in a sitting position fired at Frank McLowry as he crossed Fremont Street, and at the same instant Doc Holliday shot at him, both balls taking effect, either of which would have proved fatal, as one struck him in the right temple and the other in the left breast...

WYATT AND DOC IN JAIL
The two spent almost three weeks in jail before being released.

"In looking over this massive testimony...I find it is anything but clear."
—WELLS SPICER

THE LEGAL MACHINE

H.M. Matthews, the county coroner impanels a jury to hear evidence. On October 28, statements are taken from eight witnesses. The final coroner's verdict is a statement of the obvious: "William Clanton, Frank and Thomas McLaury, came to their deaths in the town of Tombstone on October 26, 1881, from the effects of pistol and gunshot wounds inflicted by Virgil Earp, Morgan Earp, Wyatt Earp and one Holliday—commonly called Doc Holliday." The verdict contains no "felonious intent."

The next day, October 29, Ike Clanton swears out complaints against the Earps and Holliday. This is significant in an odd way. Johnny Behan will be a major witness for the prosecution. As county sheriff, significant weight would have been added to the complaint had Behan filed the charges. It appears Johnny will only go so far on this matter. Testify—yes, but file charges—no.

The 49-year-old Wells Spicer will hear the case. Formerly from Utah, Spicer had been a mining engineer and attorney in Salt Lake City. In 1857, Spicer had defended John Lee, a Mormon Indian Agent, for his part in the infamous Mountain Meadows Massacre. Lee was found guilty for leading a group of Mormons and Indians in the slaughter of a Gentile wagon train. Spicer came to Tucson in 1878 and now serves Tombstone as judge.

Thomas Fitch, an old friend of Mark Twain's, serves as Wyatt Earp's counsel. Thomas J. Drum represents Doc.

Lyttleton Price nominally leads the prosecution. However, Ben Goodrich, a Texan hired by Clanton interests, will carry most of the case load.

DAMNED IF HE DOES, DAMNED IF HE DOESN'T
Wells Spicer is 49 years old when he hears his most famous case. Cow-boy partisans claim Spicer is crooked. Earp fans see his decision as a clear reading of the law.

STAR WITNESS

**IKE CLANTON—STILL RUNNING
FROM THE TRUTH**

From October 31 to November 30, 1881 Tombstone is held spellbound by the Spicer Hearing. All the prosecutor needs to show is "probable cause" and the case will go to trial. After a parade of witnesses make things look bad for Doc and his friends, Ike Clanton takes the stand. In cross examination, he is asked about his deal with Wyatt Earp to nab Leonard, Head and Crane for the Benson stage robbery. Overconfident, Clanton spins a yarn alleging the Earps and Holliday had "piped" away the coach booty before the stage left. Then, Leonard, Head and Crane, led by Doc, enacted a charade robbery to cover the earlier heist. When Wyatt grew worried that the trio would implicate him if caught, he approached Ike to lure the wanted men to a place where they could be murdered. Ike was offered the reward money as an incentive to betray his friends. Ike testifies he righteously refused.

The holes in his testimony are so large, they undermine the entire prosecution's case. 1) No money was missing off the Benson coach, so the tale of "piping away" funds is untrue. 2) While Ike denied, under oath, he made any deal with Wyatt he had contradicted this at the Matthew's inquest when he said, "They (the Earps) don't like me. We had a transaction—I mean, myself and the Earps—but it had nothing to do with the killing of these men." So, despite Behan's, Allen's, Claiborne's, and Fuller's testimonies, it was Ike Clanton—star witness for the prosecution—who saved the day for the defense.

LOCATION OF THE WITNESSES TO THE GUNFIGHT

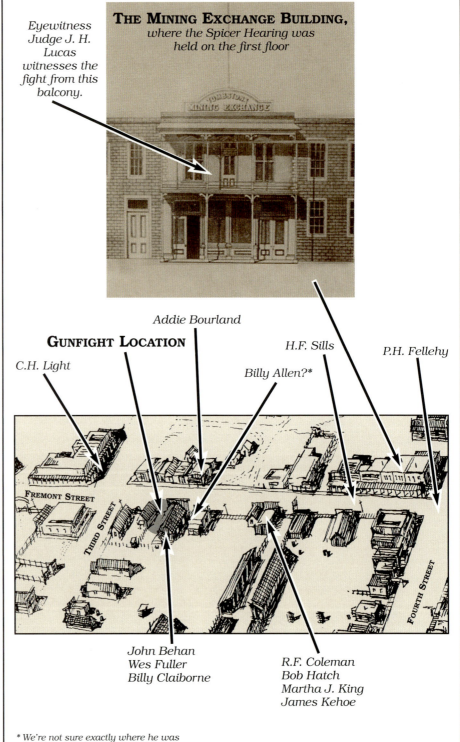

Eyewitness Judge J. H. Lucas witnesses the fight from this balcony.

THE MINING EXCHANGE BUILDING, *where the Spicer Hearing was held on the first floor*

Addie Bourland

GUNFIGHT LOCATION

C.H. Light

H.F. Sills

Billy Allen?*

P.H. Fellehy

John Behan
Wes Fuller
Billy Claiborne

R.F. Coleman
Bob Hatch
Martha J. King
James Kehoe

* We're not sure exactly where he was

"I live on the opposite side of Fremont Street from the entrance to Fly's Lodging House."
—ADDIE BOURLAND

QUESTION: *"How long did you continue to look at the parties after they met?"*

ADDIE BOURLAND: *"...until they commenced to fire, and I got up then and went to my back room."* (PHOTOS BY BBB*)

November, 1881

Because Virgil and Morgan Earp are bedridden from wounds received, only Doc and Wyatt are arrested—by Harry Woods. The two are released on bail but re-incarcerated on November 7, when W.R. McLaury moves they be remanded to Behan's custody without bail because of the damaging testimony of prosecution witnesses. They will be released again on November 24, after the testimony of H.F. Sills.

November 28, 1881

One of the last witnesses to appear is Addie Bourland. She testifies she lives across the street from Fly's. "I saw five men opposite my house, leaning against the small house west of Fly's Gallery and one man was holding a horse standing a little out from the house. I supposed them to be cow-boys, and saw four men coming down the street towards them and a man with a long coat on walked up to the man holding the horse and put a pistol to his stomach and then he, the man with the long coat on, stepped back two or three feet, and then the firing seemed to be general. That is all I saw."

To Wells Spicer, Addie Bourland is one of the most important witnesses. He actually takes it upon himself to re-interview her at her residence. He says he believes she knows more than she had testified to and recalls her to the stand.

The pivotal question is: "Please state the position in which the party called the cowboys held their hands at the time the firing commenced."

Her answer is "I didn't see anyone holding up their hands; they all seemed to be firing in general, on both sides..."

November 29, 1881

Testimony in the Wells Spicer Hearing is completed. Judge Spicer's decision is printed in the *Epitaph* two days later. In it he declares that "To constitute the crime of murder there must be proven not only the killing, but also the felonious intent...in looking over this massive testimony...I find that it is anything but clear.

"Addie Bourland, who saw distinctly the approach of the Earps...says she cannot tell which fired first—that the firing commenced at once, from both sides...and that no hands were held up; that she could have seen them if there had been. Sills asserted that the firing was almost simultaneous..."

"Considering all the testimony together, I am of the opinion that the weight of evidence sustains and corroborates the testimony of Wyatt Earp, that their demand for surrender was met by William Clanton and Frank McLaury drawing or making motions to draw their pistols. Upon this hypothesis my duty is clear...under the statutes, as well as the common law, they have a right to repel force with force...

"...the testimony of Isaac Clanton, that this tragedy was the result of a scheme on the part of the Earps to assassinate him...falls short of being a sound theory, [on] account of the great fact...that Issac Clanton was not injured at all and could have been killed first and easiest...

"...the evidence taken before me in this case, would not, in my judgment, warrant a conviction of

DID BILLY BREAKENRIDGE SAVE DOC HOLLIDAY'S LIFE?

"One dark rainy night I was tired and decided to go home, and before doing so took a walk up the street to the corner opposite the Bird Cage, to see if everything was quiet. At McKnight's store on the corner opposite the theater, as I was hugging close to the building on account of the rain, I ran up against a gun-barrel which was placed against my breast. Looking up, I saw it was Frank Stillwell.

I asked him what he was trying to do, and he said that a certain party had boasted that he was going to get him that night, and that he would not do it if he saw him first. I told him that it was too late for him to kill any one that night, that he was in enough trouble already, and to put up his gun and go home. He did as I told him, and went down the side street, and I turned back wondering whom he was after, but about the middle of the block I met Doc Holliday, who roomed a short distance up the street [on Fremont near Sixth], on his way home. It flashed through my mind that I had inadvertently saved Holliday's life that night."
—Billy Breakenridge, *Helldorado*

"There being two strong parties in the camp, of course this verdict is satisfactory to but one of them. The other accepts it with a very bad grace..."

—CLARA SPALDING BROWN
DECEMBER 7, 1881
WRITING TO THE *SAN DIEGO UNION*

THE DAISY BUSINESS

"You're a daisy if you do."
—DOC HOLLIDAY

Doc Holliday had a way with slang. Where did the daisy business come from?

"When a new slang phrase is wafted to this country, via New York, the warmth of its reception is somewhat startling. "Paralyze" has had its run, and "you paralyze me" is an exclamation that is now going quietly down to its grave. But the "daisy" business is undergoing a painful revival, for we believe it has a more venerable origin than the other. Last night on the Oakland boat we heard a young man, a clerk of some kind, remark to a companion, "she's a daisy," and a third time the vealy youth unctuously ejaculated, "They are daisies every one of them." A few moments afterwards a grave and severe looking gentleman, evidently a minister of the gospel, confided in a loud tone to another grave looking party, possibly a deacon, "I assure you it was a daisy sermon." On the other side of the deck a stock dealer was assuring a friend that "it was a daisy mine," while on the upper deck a group of fair girls were "daisying" everything at such a rate that the commonplace ferry-boat seemed a flower garden. We should like to be informed by some professor of slang the true meaning of the adjective. It is certainly the most accommodating one in the language, for it applies to everything."

—June 10, 1881.
The *San Francisco Exchange*

the defendants by trial jury of any offense whatever.

"...I conclude the performance of this duty imposed upon me by saying in the language of the Statute: 'There being no sufficient cause to believe the within named Wyatt S. Earp and John H. Holliday guilty of the offense mentioned within. I order them to be released."

December 14, 1881

Shots are fired at John Clum as he rides in a stagecoach to Benson where he will catch a train to Washington D.C. He is sure it is an assassination attempt by the cow-boys.

December 15, 1881

Virgil Earp is finally able to get out of bed and walk up town. The Earps and their friends meet in the Oriental saloon and range up to the bar for drinks. Milt Joyce, the owner, shoots off his mouth and sarcastically says, "See who's here. I expect there will be another stage robbed before morning." One of the Earps (either Wyatt or Virgil) slaps Joyce across the face, and they draw their guns. Joyce backs to the door and supposedly says, "You will not get to shoot me in the back as you have shot everyone else, and I don't think you have the nerve to shoot me when I am looking at you." He backs out the door and disappears.

December 16, 1881

Armed with a six-shooter in each hand, Milt Joyce finds the Earps in the back of a saloon and, according to Billy Breakenridge, "asked them if they wanted to fight as bad as they did the night before." Before anyone can react, Sheriff Behan comes in, and seeing the situation, grabs Joyce from behind and carries him outside and arrests him. Joyce is fined fifteen dollars and although Behan had been a close friend of Joyce's and probably saved his life, the bar owner will never forgive him for this.

December 28, 1881

At about 11:30 p.m. Virgil Earp is shot down and seriously wounded.

January 17, 1882

JOHNNY RINGO

Johnny Ringo challenges Wyatt Earp and Doc Holliday to shoot it out. Earp walks away, but Holliday puts his hand to his breast and says, "I'm your huckleberry. That's just my game." Officers separate the two and they are fined for carrying weapons.

February 11, 1882

Wyatt, Doc and Morgan are re-arrested. On February 7 Ike Clanton had Justice of the Peace J.B. Smith issue warrants for the October street fight.

February 14, 1882

Charges against the Earps and Holliday are dropped.

March 8, 1882

The Phoenix *Herald* reports that saloons along Washington Street in Phoenix are soaking their spittoons in the same irrigation ditches where most of the locals get their drinking water.

March 18, 1882

Morgan Earp is murdered. Doc goes on a rampage, busting open doors, hunting for those responsible.

March 20, 1882

The Earp entourage, including Doc, escorts Virgil and his wife Allie to Tucson on their first leg of a journey back to Colton. With Wyatt are Warren Earp, Sherm McMasters, Turkey Creek Jack Johnson, Texas Jack Vermillion

and of course Doc. Wyatt kills Frank Stillwell.

March 21, 1882

Holliday returns to Tombstone with Wyatt and the others. Warned they are now wanted for murder, the party brushes past Sheriff Behan and rides out of town.

March 22, 1882

The Earp posse shoots Florentino Cruz to pieces.

March 24, 1882

Wyatt Earp kills Curly Bill at Mescal Springs. Earp thinks Doc is actively backing his play and is disappointed to find Holliday

fleeing with the others (except Texas Jack—whose horse was shot). When Wyatt returns to the group Doc says, "Here Wyatt, you must be shot to pieces, let me help you off your horse." (In later years Wyatt would tell Stuart Lake he "always felt bad" about Doc's not backing him that day.)

April, 1882

After the Curly Bill shooting, the Earp party leaves Arizona. They go, by way of New Mexico, up into Colorado.

May 6, 1882

Congress passes, over President Chester Arthur's veto, the Chinese

---

DOC GETS THE BLAME

"Now comes Doc Holliday, as quarrelsome a man as God ever allowed to live on earth. A Georgian well-bred and well-educated, he happened in Kansas some years ago. Saving Wyatt Earp's life in Dodge City, Kansas, he earned his gratitude, and not withstanding his many bad breaks since, has always found a friend in Wyatt. Doc Holliday is responsible for all the killings, etc., in connection with what is known as the Earp-Clanton imbroglio in Arizona. He kicked up the fight, and Wyatt Earp and his brothers "stood in" with him, on the score of gratitude. Everyone in Tombstone conversant with the circumstances deprecates the killing of the McLowerys and Clanton. It's produced a feud that has driven the Earps from Arizona and virtually made outlaws of them."

—May 11, 1882, *San Francisco Examiner*

SILVER CITY, NEW MEXICO

After the Earps and Holliday flee Arizona, they land in Silver City on the evening of April 8, 1882. According to an eyewitness, they are "well mounted and armed to the teeth." Dumping their horses, they travel by stage to Rincon, where they board a north-bound train for Albuquerque and Colorado. (SILVER CITY MUSEUM)

Campbell and Hatch's, Tombstone, A.T.
(ARIZONA HISTORICAL SOCIETY LIBRARY)

MURDER OF MORGAN

"On Saturday evening, the 18th, Morgan and Wyatt Earp attended the theatre—the Lingard "Stolen Kisses" Company being here—and, after the performance was over, walked from the street to Campbell and Hatch's saloon, where they went in, and Morgan engaged in a game of pool with Hatch, Wyatt sitting looking on, in a crowded room. The table used was one at the rear of the room, and the upper half of the back door was composed of glass, the two lower panes being ground. As Morgan stood with his back to the door, two shots were fired from outside in quick succession. The first passing entirely through him and entering the leg of a bystander, George A.B. Berry. The second, evidently intended for Wyatt Earp, struck over the head of that gentleman, and did no damage. Morgan fell to the floor, and was assisted to a lounge in the card room, where he died in less than an hour. The death scene is said to have been very affecting. The man was surrounded by his brothers and their wives, whose grief was intense."

—*Clara S. Brown, reporting for the* San Diego Union, *March 31, 1882*

Exclusion Act, which bars Chinese immigrants from the U.S. for ten years.

Meanwhile, Wyatt and his men situate themselves in Gunnison. Whenever Doc drinks too much he is kept under wraps by the others. Finally Holliday and Earp argue at Pueblo and Doc goes to Denver.

May 14, 1882

Doc goes to Denver's Fair Grounds for a day at the races.

May 15, 1882

Perry Mallen, a self-appointed detective, walks up to Doc, points a brace of pistols in his direction and arrests Doc Holliday. Mallen at first claims he is a deputy sheriff from Los Angeles, California. Then he claims Doc had killed his partner, one Harry White, seven years previously. The real reason for Mallen's actions is probably the reward offered for Doc. Here is a true example of a bounty hunter. Actually Mallen hailed from Ohio. The Pueblo *Chieftain* described Perry as follows: "He is a small man, with reddish face and beard, with small ferretty eyes, and not an inviting cast of features. *(See* Police Gazette *drawing on opposite page.)*

May 22, 1882

The *Denver Republican* prints a long interview with Doc.

To protect Doc, Bat Masterson, Marshal of Trinidad, Colorado, concocts a bunco charge against Doc issued from Pueblo. This puts Doc in Bat's jurisdiction and under his protection.

Gunnison, Colorado's Virginia Avenue (DENVER PUBLIC LIBRARY, WESTERN HISTORY DEPARTMENT)

"When any of you fellows have been hunted from one end of the country to the other, as I have been, you'll understand what a bad man's reputation is built on."
—DOC HOLLIDAY

Bat Masterson dislikes Holliday immensely, but he goes out of his way to help the beleaguered dentist because Wyatt asked him to. (JEFF MOREY COLLECTION)

THE *DENVER REPUBLICAN* INTERVIEW WITH DOC

On the Sunday following his arrest, the *Denver Republican* sent a reporter to the county jail to interview Holliday. This interview, quoting Doc's own words, describing his actions and appearance, is the best picture of the man himself that can be found. The facts take quite a shellacking, but then Doc was fighting for his life—desperately acting a part before the reading public of Denver: the martyred lawman who would kill himself rather than be lynched by an outlaw gang.

"Holliday had a big reputation as a fighter, and has probably put more 'rustlers' and cowboys under the sod than any one man in the West. He has been the terror of the lawless element in Arizona, and with the Earps was the only man brave enough to face the bloodthirsty crowd, which has made the name of Arizona a stench in the nostrils of decent men. The visitor was very much surprised at Holliday's appearance, which is as different as could be from the generally conceived idea of a killer. Holliday is a slender man, not more than five feet six inches tall and would weigh perhaps 150 pounds. His face is thin and his hair sprinkled heavily with gray. His features are well formed and there is nothing remarkable in them save a well-defined look of determination from his eyes, which the veriest amateur in physiognomy could hardly mistake. His hands are small and soft like a woman's, but the work they have done is anything but womanly. The slender forefinger which has dealt the cards has dealt death to many a rustler with equal skill and quickness, and the slender wrist has proved its muscles of steel in

PERRY MALLEN

many a deadly encounter, when a quick motion of a six-shooter meant everything. Holliday was dressed neatly in black, with a colored linen shirt. The first thing noticeable about him in opening the conversation was his soft voice and modest manners. He explained the case as follows:

"'The men known as cowboys are not really cowboys. In the early days the real cowboys, who were wild and reckless, gained a great deal of notoriety. After they passed out their places were taken by a gang of murderers, stage robbers and thieves, who were refugees from justice from the Eastern States. The proper name for them is Rustlers. They ran the country down there and so terrorized the country that no man dared say anything against them. Trouble first arose with them by the killing of Marshal White by Curly Bill. Marshal White fell into my arms when he was shot and I arrested Curly Bill. The trouble then is familiar to all.'

"'Do you apprehend trouble when you are taken back?' asked the visitor.

"Holliday paused for a minute and gazed earnestly out of the window of Jailer Lambert's room into the rain outside and then said slowly, 'If I am taken back to Arizona, that is the last of Holliday.' After a pause he explained this by saying, 'We hunted the Rustlers, and they all hate us. John Behan, Sheriff of Cochise County, is one of the gang, and a deadly enemy of mine, who would give any money to have me killed. It is almost certain that he instigated the assassination of Morgan Earp. Should he get me in his power my life would not be worth much.'

"'But Sheriff Paul, of Tucson, will take you to that place, will he not?'

"'Yes, and there lies my only chance for safety. I would never go to Tombstone. I'd make an attempt to escape right outside this jail and get killed by a decent man. I would rather do that than be hung by those robbers there.'

"'Cannot Paul protect you?'

"'I'm afraid not. He is a good man, but I am afraid he cannot protect me. The jail is a little tumble-down affair, which a few men can push over, and a few cans of oil thrown upon it would cause it to burn up in a flash, and either burn a prisoner to death or drive him out to be shot down. That will be my fate.'

"'Haven't you friends there who would rally to your assistance?'

"'Yes, the respectable element will stand by me, but they are all intimidated and unorganized. They will never do anything until some respectable citizen is shot down, when the people will rise and clean them out, as they did at Fort Griffin, where twenty-four men were hung on one tree when I was there. The Tombstone Rustlers are part of the Fort Griffin gang.'

"'You are charged with killing Frank Stillwell. What do you know about that affair?'

"'I know that Stillwell was a stage robber, and one of Morgan Earp's assassins, and that he was killed near Tucson, but I do not know that I am in any way responsible for his death. I know that he robbed a stage, from the fact that he gave the money to a friend of mine to keep, and I know that he helped in the assassination of Morgan Earp, and he was seen running from the scene by several responsible citizens. Pete Spence was with them, and I am morally certain that Sheriff Behan investigated [instigated?] the assassination. He did it for two reasons. One was that he was afraid of and hated Morgan Earp, who had quarreled with and insulted him several times. He feared Earp and had every inducement to kill him. A word further about this man Behan. I have known him a long time. He first ran against me when I was running a faro bank, when he started a quarrel in my house, and I stopped him and refused to let him play any more. We were enemies after that. In the quarrel I told him in the presence of a crowd that he was gambling with money which I had given his woman. This story got out and caused him trouble. He always hated me after that, and would spend money to have me killed. He has always stood in with the Rustlers and taken his share of their plunder, and in consequence he is in their power, and must do as they say. This is shown by the fact that he has five Rustlers under him as deputies. One of these men is John Ringo, who jumped on the stage of the variety theater in Tombstone one night about three weeks ago, and took

all the jewels from the proprietor's wife in full view of the audience. These are the men who want me and that is the kind of country I am going back to for my health.'

"'It's a nice, sociable country, I must admit,' responded the visitor, who ran over mentally all the terrible outrages which had been committed of late by the noted Rustlers, including a train robbery or two and several stage robberies. Holliday, in response to a question, then turned his attention to Mallen, the officer who followed him and caused his arrest here.

"'The first time I met him,' said Holliday, 'was in Pueblo just before I came to Denver. He approached me in a variety theater and introducing himself said he wanted to do me a favor in return for saving his life in Santa Fe once. I told him I would be very thankful for any favor he wanted to show me, but he must be mistaken about my saving his life in Santa Fe, as I had never been there. He did not reply to this, but told me that he had just come up on the train with Josh Stillwell, a brother of Frank Stillwell, whom I was supposed to have killed, and that he had threatened to shoot me on sight. I thanked him for his information, and he replied, "If you give me away I will kill you." I told him I wasn't travelling around the country giving people away, and he left me. I met him in a saloon a few days afterwards, and asked the barkeeper who he was. He told me that Mallen represented that he was a ranchman, who had sold out in the lower country, and was looking for a location, upon the strength of which he borrowed $8 at one time, and $2 at another. I met the barkeeper several times afterwards, and he told me that the money had never been paid. I then considered that there was no truth in his story which he had told to me.

"'The next time I saw him was in Denver, when he dropped his guns

on me and caused my arrest. Paul does not know him, and I believe he is a crank. He acted like one at Pueblo, when he took down his clothes and showed a mark which he said was a bullet wound, but which was the mark of disease. I laughed in his face, the thing being so funny that I couldn't help it.

"'On thing which Mallen tells gives him away bad. He said in your paper that he was standing alongside Curly bill when the latter was killed. The facts are these: We were out one day after a party of outlaws, and about 3 o'clock on a warm day after a long and dry ride from the San Pedro river, we approached a spring which was situated in a hollow. As we did so, eight Rustlers rose up from behind the bank and poured from thirty-five to forty shots into us. Our escape was miraculous. The shots cut our clothes and saddles and killed one horse, but did not hit us. I think we would have been all killed if God Almighty wasn't on our side. Wyatt Earp turned loose with a shot-gun and killed Curly Bill. The eight men in the gang which attacked us were all outlaws, for each of whom a big reward has been offered. They were such men as Curly Bill, Pete Spencer and Pony Deal, all of them wanted by the authorities and Wells, Fargo & Co. Pony Deal, I am told, was killed a few days ago on the railroad by soldiers. If Mallen was alongside of Curly Bill when he was killed, he was with one of the worst gangs of murderers and robbers in the country.'

"'Where are the Earps?'

"'In Colorado, over in the Gunnison, I believe.'

"'Didn't you have a quarrel with them in Pueblo a few weeks ago?'

"'We had a little misunderstanding, but it didn't amount to much.'

"'Would they help you now?'

"'Yes, all they could; but they are wanted themselves, and of

THE GUNFIGHTER AND THE NUN

(PHOTO BY BBB*)

As children, John Henry Holliday, and his cousin Mattie, became strong friends. Mattie was the daughter of Doc's uncle, Robert Kennedy Holliday, and Aunt Mary Anne Fitzgerald. Mattie was born on December 14, 1849 at Fayetteville, Georgia. Her high school education was received at Clayton High School in Jansboro. Family sources claim Mattie was the one member of the family Doc kept in continual touch with. On October 1, 1883, Mattie entered St. Vincent's Catholic convent in Savannah, Georgia. She assumed the name, Sister Mary Melanie, and spent her life as a teacher and Sister Superior. Her gentle and kindly spirit was so wildly respected, Margaret Mitchell is said to have patterned the sweet-natured "Melanie" in "Gone With The Wind" after Doc's cousin. Sister Mary Melanie died at St. Joseph's Infirmary in Atlanta, Georgia on April 19, 1939.

Over the years, many have thought Doc and his cousin were romantically involved. Pat Jahns claimed such was the case in her book, "The Frontier World of Doc Holliday." Jahns, however, offered no documentation for the claim and the family strongly disputes the allegation.

The most painful revelation, for historians, has to do with Doc's letters. Family members who read them say they were lengthy and highly literate accounts of Doc's view of the opening of the frontier. Doc Holliday had an awareness of history and his correspondence is said to have reflected his classical education. Sister Melanie, herself, told her family that had she not destroyed some of Doc's correspondence, the "world would have known a different man from the one of Western fame." Did Sister Melanie destroy some or all of the letters? Some say a member of her family burnt the rest as having been inappropriate for a Catholic nun to receive. However, there's always hope that somewhere, someone has a trunk full of the lost letters of Doc Holliday.

course couldn't go back with me without putting themselves in danger, without doing me any good.'

"Holliday in conclusion said that Mallen's claim that he, Holliday, had killed his partner in Utah, was false, as at the very time Mallen claims the killing was done, the speaker was here in Denver dealing for Charley Foster, in Babbitt's house, where Ed Chase is now located. Holliday further says he was never in Utah. After leaving Denver he went to Dodge City, Kansas, where he stayed some time, going to Arizona from there. In going back he said he would be safe until he reached a point below Albuquerque and that it would not be healthy for Mallen to go on the same train....

"Today in the District Court of Arapahoe County the writ of habeas corpus will come up. The requisition will arrive today. As it is pretty well assured that Holliday will be killed if taken back, the case will be thoroughly investigated before a requisition will be allowed."

Bob Paul had arrived armed with warrants, only to find that Wyatt and Warren were several hundred miles away and Doc was the sole Arizonan in the Denver jail. The requisition was delayed to exasperation. That Doc and the Earps escaped being taken back to Arizona in leg-irons is due to the red tape which fouled up the entire proceeding as much as to Perry Mallen's odd behavior.

An interview with Bob Paul, who "is of large physique, weighing probably two hundred pounds, [and] has a frank, open countenance," shows that he was somewhat on the fence as to the position of Doc and his friends. Asked if Doc was a member of the Earp gang, Paul said, "He was, and in fact was one of the leaders. The so-called Earp gang, or faction, if you please, was composed entirely of gamblers who preyed upon the cowboys, and at the same time in order to keep up a show of having a legitimate calling, was organized into a sort of vigilance committee, and some of them, including Holliday, had United States Marshal's commissions."

"'Was Holliday regarded as a desperate character?'

"'Not by any means. He was always decently peaceable, though his powers when engaged in following his ostensible calling, furthering the ends of justice, made him a terror to the criminal classes of Arizona.'"

On May 23, 1882, the Pueblo *Chieftain* said: "Mallen, the man who arrested 'Doc' Holliday in Denver recently, has at last admitted that his story of a seven-years hunt for his man was a fabrication. The indications are at present that Holliday will be acquitted in Denver and that he will not be taken back to Arizona."

But the very next day the *Rocky Mountain News* carried: "Sheriff Paul received a telegram yesterday from the Secretary of Arizona Territory stating that the requisition had been forwarded from Tucson last Friday, hence it is expected momentarily. The case has begun to look very dark for Holliday, and it is nearly settled that he will have to go back to Tucson with Sheriff Paul who guarantees him protection against violence. It is not strange, however, that he should object to going back for trial as he left there to avoid this inconvenience."

Perry Mallen turned up again in the *Rocky Mountain News* on May 25, 1882, stating that Johnny Behan had offered a $500 reward for Doc and that the Cochise County commissioners had offered $1000 for him. The more he attempted to justify his actions, the more it looked as if these rewards alone were responsible for Doc being in jail.

The requisition finally arrived and was formally presented to Governor Pitkin on Friday, May 26, 1882. It had been put to the governor pretty strongly that Holliday stood no chance of anything even resembling justice if he was returned to Arizona and on the following Monday he was

THE TELLER HOUSE, UPSTAIRS
One of Colorado's most infamous sporting houses in the 1880s.

THE GAMBLER'S UNIFORM

Doc is a snappy dresser as are most western sporting men. The dapper gent (right) is wearing the uniform of the well dressed gambler; top coat, deerskin gloves and derby.

Leadville, Colorado (STATE HISTORICAL SOCIETY OF COLORADO LIBRARY)

released into the custody of the Pueblo marshal.

The Pueblo *Chieftain* for June 1, 1882, carried: "'Doc' Holliday is in the city, and his troubles, for the present, are apparently over with. Yesterday morning he appeared before Justice McBride upon a charge of having swindled a man out of one hundred dollars—a complaint entered against him just after he went to Denver. He waived examination and was bound over to appear before the District Court, providing a true bill was found against him. He was placed under bonds of $300, which he furnished, thus securing his liberty. He will remain in this city until his case is finally disposed of. He has no fears of the outcome.... The *Cincinnati Enquirer*, of Sunday, contained over a column of twaddle devoted to this case. A biographical sketch of the principal was included, in which it was made to appear that he has in his time killed over fifty men, and that Jesse James is a saint compared to him. The article in question has caused much amusement among Holliday's friends."

Mr. Perry Mallen vanished from Denver under somewhat of a cloud and in possession of $161 and a valuable revolver that didn't belong to him. He was arrested in Pittsburgh and held for requisition from there by the Colorado authorities, but I was unable to discover the final disposition of his case.

Doc settled down to a quiet and routine existence as a gambler in South Pueblo. The romance of his story made him a well-known local character, a tame killer to brag about, just as Trinidad had Bat Masterson to boast about to visiting easterners. He went to court again on July 18, 1882, charged with larceny, but got his case continued. It was continued on into infinity, although he was careful to keep himself under indictment so that the Arizona authorities couldn't grab him.

Pueblo, Holliday felt, was a lucky town.

June 1, 1882

Doc is in custody in Pueblo on charges of swindling a man of $100. The case is continued continually just to give Doc safe haven in Colorado.

When Sheriff Spangler telegraphs Johnny Behan and Bob Paul that he has Holliday and the Earps in jail, Gov. Tritle of Arizona selects Paul to bring Doc back. Paul gets the requisition from the Governor and goes up to Denver. Before Paul arrives Bat Masterson pleads Doc's case and Wyatt's friend Horace Tabor also intercedes.

This is the Gambling Room of the Pioneer Saloon at Leadville, Colorado. (WESTERN HISTORY COLLECTION, DENVER PUBLIC LIBRARY)

THE MYSTERIOUS DEATH OF JOHNNY RINGO

From the *Daily Epitaph* July 18, 1882:

His Body Found in Morse's Canyon—Probable Suicide

Sunday evening intelligence reached this city of the finding of the dead body of John Ringo near the mouth of Morse's canyon in the Chiricahua mountains on Friday afternoon. There was few men in Cochise County, or Southern Arizona better known. He was recognized by friends and foes as a recklessly brave man, who would go any distance, or undergo any hardship to serve a friend or punish an enemy. While undoubtedly reckless, he was far from being a desperado, and we know of no murder being laid to his charge. Friends and foes are unanimous in the opinion that he was a strictly honorable man in all his dealings, and that his word was as good as his bond. Many

people who were intimately acquainted with him in life, have serious doubts that he took his own life, while an equally large number say that he frequently threatened to commit suicide, and that event was expected at any time. The circumstances of the case hardly leave any room for doubt as to his own self destruction. He was about 200 feet from water, and was acquainted with every inch of the country, so that it was almost impossible for him to loose himself. He was found in the midst of a clump of oaks, springing from the same stem, but diverging outward so as to leave an open space in the centre. On top of the main stem and between the spreading boughs, was a large stone and on this pedestal he was found sitting, with his body leaning backward and resting against a tree. He was found by a man named John Yost, who was acquainted with him for years, both in this Territory and Texas. Yost is working for Sorgum Smith, and was employed hauling wood. He was driving a team along the road, and noticed a man in the

midst of the clump of trees, apparently asleep. He passed on without further investigation, but on looking back, saw his dog smelling of the man's face and snorting. This excited curiosity, so he stopped the team, alighted, and proceeded to investigate. He found the lifeless body of John Ringo, with a hole large enough to admit two fingers about half way between the right eye and ear, and a hole correspondingly large on the top of his head, doubtless the outlet of the fatal bullet. The revolver was firmly clenched in his hand, which is almost conclusive evidence that death was instantaneous. His rifle rested against a tree and one of his cartridge belts was turned upside down. Yost immediately gave the alarm and in about fifteen minutes eleven men were on the spot. There was a bullet hole on the top of the head on the left side. There is apparently, a part of the scalp gone, including a small portion of the forehead and part of the hair. This looks as if cut out by a knife. These are the only marks of violence visible on the

JOHN RINGO

DID DOC KILL JOHNNY RINGO?

Dramatic structure yearns to see the matter settled. However, different sources have Doc in court on July 11. Ringo met his death on July 11, 1882 and his body was found on the 13th. Whatever else Doc was capable of, he wasn't able to cover the miles between Pueblo and West Turkey Creek Canyon quick enough to have delighted in Ringo's last seconds of life.

body. Several of the undersigned identify the body as that of John Ringo, well known in Tombstone. He was dressed in light hat, blue shirt, vest, pants and drawers. On his feet were a pair of hose and an undershirt torn up so as to protect his feet. He had evidently traveled but a short distance in this foot-gear. His revolver he grasped in his right hand, his rifle resting against the tree close to him. He had on two cartridge belts, the belt for revolver cartridges being buckled on upside down. The undernoted property was found with him and on his person: 1 Colt's revolver, Calibre 45... 1 Winchester rifle octagon barrel, calibre 45, model 1876, No. 21,896, containing a cartridge in the breech and ten in the magazine; 1 cartridge belt, containing 9 rifle cartridges; 1 cartridge belt, containing 2 revolver cartridges; 1 silver watch of American Watch Company, No. 9339 with silver chain attached; two dollars and sixty cents ($2.60) in money, 6 pistol cartridges in pocket; 5 shirt studs; 1 small pocket knife; 1 tobacco pipe; 1 comb; 1 block matches; 1 small piece tobacco. There is also a portion of a letter from Messer. Herford & Zabriskie, attorneys at law, Tucson, to the deceased, John Ringo...The body of the deceased was buried close to where it was found.

The inmates of Smith's house heard a shot about three o'clock Thursday evening, and it is more than likely that that is the time the rash deed was done. He was on an extended jamboree the last time he was in this city, and only left here ten days ago... He was subject to frequent fits of melancholy and had an abnormal fear of being killed. Two weeks ago last Sunday in conversing with the writer, he said he was as certain of being killed, as he was of being living then. He said he might run along for a couple of years more, and may not last two days...Many friends will mourn him, and many others will take secret delight in learning of his death.

July 11, 1882

Doc makes a court appearance in Pueblo—his lawyer could have made an appearance without Doc, but there's no evidence that happened.—This pretty much rules out Doc as a suspect in the death of John Ringo as that cowboy is killed the same day.

July 29, 1882

The Weekly *Epitaph* runs a story under the headline "A Tough Story." The sub-head is "Doc Holliday takes in a reporter." The old guard in Tombstone has changed and the new editor of the *Epitaph*, Sam Purdy, makes it clear whose side he's on as he takes Doc and the *Denver Republican* to task and portrays the article as pure bunk.

1883 (Month and day not known with precision.)

Doc goes to Leadville where he gets work as a faro dealer for Cy Allen at the Monarch saloon at 320 Harrison Ave. Doc's old nemesis from Tombstone—Johnny Tyler is—also in town and the old animosities still burn. Tyler puts men up to taunt Doc and after triggering Holliday's temper, steps back, giving the world the appearance Doc is a crazy man. Finally, Cy Allen fires Doc.

Broke, sick and usually drunk, Holliday hits rock bottom. Mannie Hyman, owner of Hyman's saloon at 316 Harrison, gives Doc a room. After some poker winnings give him hope again, Doc moves to 219

MANNIE HYMAN

West Third. However, he makes the mistake of borrowing five dollars from another old Tombstoner, Billy Allen. When he doesn't get his money back Allen decides to rub it in the little invalid's face.

August 19, 1884

According to Doc's friends, Billy Allen gives Doc until noon of the 19th to pay up. If he does not receive his due funds, he (Allen) is going to thump Doc. Holliday is in Hyman's saloon when Allen enters. Immediately Doc pulls a cut-off Colt's Single Action .44 and lets Billy have a near-death experience. The first shot hits above Allen, who then turns to exit and reconsiders. The quick spin trips up Billy who flops on the floor when a second shot hits him in the right arm. Before Doc can fire again Capt. Bradbury of the City Police runs in and yanks Doc's gun from his hand.

Doc's friends come up with $8,000 in bail money. Holliday has a short, sweet streak of good fortune at the poker table and gets his pocket watch and jewelry out of 'soak.'

March 27, 1885

Doc's trial for the shooting of Billy Allen starts. After telling of his long-standing trouble with Johnny Tyler and how Billy Allen is one of Tyler's cronies, Doc is acquitted and ordered to leave town. He makes his way back to Denver.

1886

Doc is 34, white-haired, stooped-over and needs a cane to *(continued on page 102)*

(continued on page 102)

MIRROR IMAGE?

Bat Masterson thought he was seeing double. Once when Wyatt and Josephine Earp visited him in Denver, Masterson introduced them to actress Jeffreys Lewis (above). Bat was thunderstruck by the resemblance between the two beauties. Lewis was a well-known New York actress who performed into the 20th century. That Josephine would recount the tale, years later, indicates that she was flattered.

THE PALACE THEATER, IN DENVER, 1882
The very reverent Henry Martyn Hart called it "a death trap to young men, a foul den of vice and corruption." Doc, Wyatt and Bat all agreed and went there every chance they could. In fact, Bat Masterson met his wife, Emma at the Palace. The gambling room was operated by twenty-five dealers and could accommodate 200 players. A gigantic gas chandelier, in the ballroom, dazzled patrons with reflective lights from 500 glass prisms.
(COURTESY DENVER PUBLIC LIBRARY, WESTERN HISTORY DEPARTMENT)

RIDING THE RAILS

The Rio Grande Railroad winds its way toward Silverton, through the precipitous Animas Canyon, deep in the San Juan mountains. Doc rode many of Colorado's narrow gauge trains as he made his way on the gambling circuit. Note the fisherman on the river of lost souls.

DOC ON THE ROCKS, 1885

(ILLUSTRATION OF DOC, BBB)

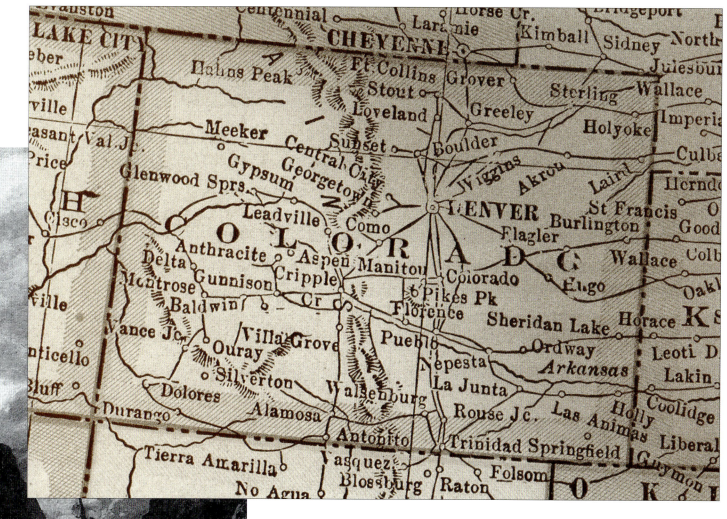

DOC BANGS AROUND COLORADO

Because of the movies we think of Doc Holliday and Wyatt Earp as inseparable. However, after leaving Arizona, in 1882, they quarreled—about what, we don't know—and spilt up. Doc lives a full five years longer in Colorado. From Denver to Silverton, from Leadville to Trinidad, Doc barely manages to stay afloat, and his health deteriorates. The high altitude is no help and his drinking affects his mind. His focus is gone. Kate later claims she was with him in these years, but that's doubtful as she doesn't appear in records as living with him. Doc has friends, but no soulmate. Some think he has no soul. Times are hard and the future offers nothing to dream of. The mind drifts back to the past. Doc reflects and writes letters to his cousin—Sister Mary Melanie. Sometimes death can be greeted like the closing of a sore wound.

walk. The reform movement is sweeping Denver in a moral fever to rid mankind of its only true source of pleasure-namely vice. The anti-gambling sentiment is making life difficult for men like Holliday; his era is nearing its end.

August 4, 1886

Doc is arrested for vagrancy. He continues the case, goes to Pueblo again for a short time, but that burg is dead. He then travels back to Leadville, where he heard of the healthful benefits of the hot springs at Glenwood Springs. The vapors there will cure you or kill you. One last hope to hold on to life.

May, 1886

Doc arrives in Glenwood Springs and ensconces himself at the Glenwood Hotel. He has to be helped off the train. After a few sessions in the baths, he notices sores on his body. His pulmonary tuberculosis has developed into galloping consumption (military tuberculosis) which attacks the whole body. He becomes bedridden and has his meals brought up to his room, always greeting the bell boy with a brace of revolvers. According to Mrs. Cason, Josephine Earp claims she and Wyatt visit Doc the day before Holliday finally dies. Before he goes out he takes hold of the Catholic religion to satisfy his cousin Mattie—now Sister Mary Melanie.

BICYCLIST - CA. 1887

A.W. Dennis was a Colorado photographer who set up shop, in Glenwood Springs, for one year only—1887. Among the photos with his marking is the above image. Wyatt Earp is said to have given it to a lawman friend in later years, identifying it as Doc Holliday's last picture. (CRAIG FOUTS COLLECTION)

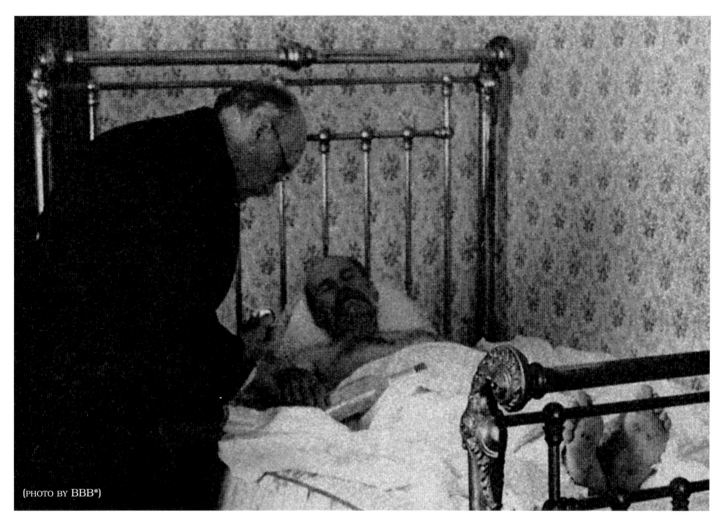

(PHOTO BY BBB*)

THE MYTHICAL SANITARIUM

For some reason, the movies like to have Doc die in a sanitarium. There never was a sanitarium. Glenwood Springs was a health resort. The hot springs boasted of promised healing powers far in excess of reality. Unfortunately, Doc's sessions in the baths exposed him to sulfuric fumes, which ate into his lung tissue. His sorry state was aggravated and he became bedridden in a room at the Hotel Glenwood. In later years one old timer claimed to have been a bellboy who took meals up to the dying gunslinger. He claimed Holliday always greeted him with a brace of big pistols.

THE HOTEL GLENWOOD
Where Doc Holliday died.

Gallons of whiskey had failed to make a dent. An untold number of bullets had missed their mark. It was the cure that killed him.

November 8, 1887

For the last two weeks he has been delirious. This morning he awakens and asks for a tumbler of whiskey. He drinks it down "with deliberate satisfaction." At ten o'clock in the morning, he dies of consumption (the shredded walls of his lungs couldn't keep the water from rising in them—so he literally drowned). His last words are a matter of debate. Kate said they were, "Well, I'm going just as I told them—the bugs would get me before the worms did." Legend has it though that the peacefulness of the final moment surprised him. "I'll be damned," he said, "This is funny!" For someone who went out of his way to die with his boots on, it was.

THE FINAL JOKE

Humor, especially black humor, seemed to follow the good doctor—even in death.

When Doc was dying, he went out under the banner of two different faiths. To Father Ed Downey, a Catholic priest, Doc claimed he had already been baptized a Catholic (and the local paper reported Doc was baptized even though there is no record of it). Meanwhile, to the Presbyterian minister, W. S. Rudolph, Doc claimed he had been raised and baptized a Presbyterian. Both faiths claimed him but there's little doubt who got him.

Reverend Rudolph gave the funeral address. The Glenwood Springs paper said that he was buried in Linwood Cemetery, November 8, at 4 p.m. "in the presence of many friends." (They would have to be good friends, because he was buried on the same day he died.) The paper also went on to say, "That 'Doc' Holliday had his faults none will attempt to deny: but who among us had not, and who shall be the judge of these things."

"He had only one correspondent among his relatives—a cousin, a Sister of Charity [Mary Melanie], in Atlanta, Georgia. She will be notified of his death, and will in turn advise any other relatives he may have living."

What the paper didn't mention is that the winter weather prevented the hearst from making it up the steep road to Linwood Cemetery, which sits on a high mesa. Doc was buried at the foot of the mesa until he could be transferred. According to townsfolk he never was. As the years went by, Glenwood Springs grew outward and today, Doc lies buried in someone's backyard.

Without a doubt he's laughing. He was a backdoor man in life and in death he became a backyard man.

Doc's headstone in Linwood Cemetery. In addition to the date of his birth being wrong (he was born in 1851), there's one other small detail—his body isn't there.

The town of Glenwood Springs, looking north from Doc's grave. One of the houses in this photo may have a legend in their garden.

The steep trail going up to Linwood cemetery. It's easy to see how the hearst might not make it to the top if it was icy or muddy.

A view of Tombstone, from the courthouse roof taken in 1905. The close-up (below) is taken from this photo.

GUNFIGHT SITE REVISITED

Here is another early view of the gunfight site. Taken 24 years after the shootout, Fly's lodging house and gallery are still clearly visible. Note the rear door Ike Clanton scampered through in his flight from the Earps and Doc Holliday. Across the street is the small adobe building Frank McLaury fell in front of. To the right of it is Addie Bourland's house—directly across from Fly's. C.S. Fly's building was finally destroyed by fire in 1912. Today it is taken as a matter of fact that the shootout didn't happen at the O.K. Corral. But history is fickle. Just when the truth seems clear, the fog rises again. Some now claim that at the time of the shooting, John Montgomery was leasing the vacant lot as an alternative to the rear entrance to the O.K. Corral. If true, this would help explain why so many old-timers claimed the shooting occurred at the O.K. Corral's rear gate.

The adobe house Frank McLaury died in front of

Addie Bourland's

Fly's

The door Ike Clanton ran through

The (above) photo of the gunfight site was taken in 1905 from the roof of the courthouse. Here is a clear view of the gunfight location, before Fly's burned down in 1912. Across the street we can clearly see the adobe house that Frank McLaury fell near. On its right is the house from which Addie Bourland witnessed the shooting.

Fly's is completely destroyed by fire in 1912. No one knows how many priceless photos were lost. With the resurgence of interest in the gunfight, the site was rebuilt in the early 60s using the top two photos for reference.

"The inmates of every house in town were greatly startled by the sudden report of fire arms, about 3 p.m., discharged with such lightening-like rapidity that it could be compared only to the explosion of a bunch of fire crackers."

—CLARA S. BROWN
OCT. 29, 1881

FADE TO BLACK

As the years go by, authors and publishers begin to monkey with the existing images of Doc and Wyatt. In real life, both men were ashe blondes and their photos bear this out. But as photo retouchers began to "enhance" their portraits, a curious evolution happened. Intentionally (or unintentionally), Wyatt's mustache darkens and takes on a Snidely Whiplash twirl. His slicked-back hair also darkens. Likewise, Doc's hair and mustache become a sinister black to match his "haunted eyes." And even though Doc preferred to dress in stylish grays, he will be portrayed in countless movies draped in black. From this distortion, the prototype of the Old West Gunfighter is born or bastardized, depending on how you look at it. The resulting image is a cliche, immediately recognized around the world—four tall, dark, black-frocked men with black string ties who, when standing together, meld into a dark unit, part preacher, part killer—spitting black bullets from pearl handled guns—a Frontier Fighting Machine.

Jim Earle's cover illustration for "The Earps Talk" by Alford E. Turner.

DOC BEFORE

DOC AFTER

WYATT BEFORE

WYATT AFTER

"So you see they are all dead and gone except me."
—BIG NOSE KATE,
MARCH 19, 1940

BIG NOSE KATE PLAYS HER LAST HAND

After Doc departed, she knocked around Arizona—running a "hotel" in Globe, marrying a blacksmith named George M. Cummings in 1888 and moving to Bisbee. In 1899 she dumped Cummings (because he drank too much), kept his name, and went to work at another "hotel" in the small railroad town of Cochise. At the turn of the century she was hired to keep house for John J. Howard at Dos Cabezas, which she did until his death in 1930. Howard left her a small amount of property which she promptly sold.

A year later, in January of 1931, Kate applied for admission to the Pioneer's Home in Prescott declaring: "At present I am a county ward...I am past eighty

(PHOTO BY BBB*)

Mary K. Cummings (second from left) *age 80, and Mrs. Alexander Haroney, 1930*
(BOYER COLLECTION, SHARLOT HALL MUSEUM LIBRARY/ARCHIVES, PRESCOTT, ARIZONA)

years old my health is not best. I was in the county hospital nearly all summer...I was advised not to live alone; but I have no income to pay any one to stay with me..."

She was admitted the same year and lived her final nine years there as Mary K. Cummings.

Kate—or Mary, as she was then going by—became angered with the publication of Walter Noble Burns' "Tombstone" (1927) and Stuart Lakes' "Wyatt Earp: Frontier Marshal" (1931). She was not alone. Many of the old-timers at the home were resentful of what they viewed as embellished and fictionalized accounts of their lives that glorified violence and gunplay.

However, she was interested in all the money she believed the authors were making, and she became convinced that she could cash in and tell her story, as Mrs. Mary Holliday.

With the help of a young graduate student at the University of Arizona (A.W. Bork, later Dr. Bork) she tried numerous times to interest the *Saturday Evening Post*, Collier's and other magazines in her story. None were interested.

What follows is a letter to her niece, Mrs. Lillian Lane Raffert, dated March 18, 1940. Although the letter leaves no doubt as to why the magazines weren't interested, it does cast new light on Doc, Wyatt and the gunfight.

The hand-written letter is transcribed here as she wrote it, but we have corrected some spelling and added punctuation to facilitate understanding. Brackets are the author's:

Pioneers Home
Prescott Arizona
Mar 18, 1940

My Dear Niece Lillie,

I received your welcome just four days ago, I am very glad to hear from you. This sick spell left me very shaky, my hands shake so, it is hard for me to write, I am feeling some better today I don't think I will get thoroughly over it,

Pioneer Home, Prescott, Arizona, 1935 (SHARLOT HALL MUSEUM LIBRARY/ARCHIVES, PRESCOTT, ARIZONA)

though I am well taken care of, nurses are all very kind to me, so I have nothing to complain of, only I am so weak that I have to stop writing to rest my hands at every few lines I write. To be sick in bed five weeks is enough to make any one weak at my age;

I can't tell you the population of Prescott but Prescott is a big city, I will find out and let you know next time I write

Doc and I met Wyatt Earp in fall of 1875 in Dodge City in 1876, Wyatt, Earp and Doc were just aquaintances at that time. Doc and I were in Dodge we were in Dodge City five weeks and went to Las Vegas, we lived in Las Vegas over two years Doc was practicing dentistry in Las Vegas, in 1879 Doc met Wyatt Earp in Las Vegas again in 1879 Wyatt Earp was on his way to Arizona, he got Doc.

and I to go with him, Wyatt had his wife, and Brother James and his wife and Daughter with him that made seven of us in the outfit. We arrived in Prescott in November, Doc and I went to a hotel, Virgil Earp the oldest Brother was already in Prescott was there two years ahead of us. It was just about the boom of Tombstone, Doc and I stayed in Prescott until the fall of 1880. The Earps went to Tombstone, the Earp brothers and family went to Tombstone early in the spring of 1880, Doc and I went to Tombstone in fall of 1881 then we went to Tombstone; I did not like it in Tombstone I went to Globe, I wanted Doc to go with me, the Earps had such power I could not get Doc away from them. I used to get letters from Doc to come to Tombstone, begging to pay him a

visit, I went to see him three times; when I went to Globe I had about five hundred dollars I bought out a hotel on time every time I went to visit Doc I had to pay a friend to look after my interests in the hotel, at that time Doc had a room at a Mrs. Fly's photograph gallery. The fiesta was on at Tucson, Doc asked if I would like to go to see the fiesta in Tucson, I said yes, so we went to Tucson. The next while we were at the park, Morgan Earp came to Tucson, came to the park, tapped Doc on the shoulder and said, Doc we want you in Tombstone tomorrow, better go up this evening. Neither of them wanted me to go with them, Doc wanted to take me back to the hotel I insisted on going back with them Doc said you can't stand the ride on a buck board from Benson to Tombstone, I said I can stand what ever you

Arizona Pioneers, residents and staff of the Arizona Pioneers Home, line up for a portrait in the 1930s. Big Nose Kate may very well be in this photo...can you spot her? (SHARLOT HALL MUSEUM LIBRARY/ARCHIVES, PRESCOTT, ARIZONA)

can, so we went back to Tombstone, he left me at his room and he went with Morgan Earp. I did not see him again till half past one in the morning, I got up next morning before Doc did. Our door opened in to the hall, our door was partly open, I saw a man come in with his head bandaged and a rifle in his hand he went to the dining and asked Mrs Fly if Doc Holliday was there, Mrs Fly said she didn't know. Mrs. Fly told me that Ike Clanton was there looking for Doc, I told Doc, Ike Clanton was looking for him. Doc said, if God will let me live to get my clothes on, he shall see me. With that he got up dressed and went out, as he went out, he said, I may not be back to take you to breakfast so you better go alone. I didn't go to breakfast, I don't remember of eating anything that day. Theres a vacant lot

between the corner and Mrs. Fly's home. I saw four men coming from the livery stable on Allen Street coming to the vacant lot, almost at the same time I saw Virgil Earp, Wyatt, Morgan Earp and Doc Holliday coming to the vacant lot from Fremont street. They stood ten feet apart when the shooting began, Ike Clanton ran and left his young Brother Billy. I saw Doc fall but he was up as quick as he fell. Something went wrong with his rifle, he threw his rifle on the ground and pulled out his six shooter. Every shot he fired got a man, Billy Clanton was killed as were the two McLaurys. Virgil and Morgan Earp were killed Doc had a grazed right hip Virge and Morgan Earp get well. It is foolish to think that a cow rustler gun man can come up to a city gun man in a gun fight; the sheriff

knew all about this fight coming off, he put on his big cow hat and rode out of the town, three days after this killing [Doc and Wyatt] gave themselves up. The jailer locked them up for one day and night when two business went on their bonds, every body knew these cow rustlers came to town to kill the Earps and Doc Holliday. They had a trial, they were aquitted; the Earps went to their parents, Doc holliday went to Glenwood Springs Colo, he is buried there. Warren Earp the youngest Brother was killed at Willcox and is buried there at the expense of Cochise County. Virgil died Verginia [sic] Nevada. Wyatt Earp died in Los Angeles Calif. J. H. Doc Holliday died in Glenwood Springs Colo. So you see they are all dead and gone except me;

There are so many who claim

they saw that shooting on Allen Street, it was not on Allen street but nearer to Fremont Street in an open lot, some that were not even born at that time. Here is what happened in Globe one morning, A Merchant Mrs Baily brought a man in for breakfast after breakfast hours, I waited on him because my girl was doing up the rooms, they got to talking about Tombstone, some how Doc and I were mentioned, he told Mr Baily that Doc took me to New Mexico and killed me up in the mountains and that he helped to bury me. I said the poor woman, Mr Baily and I laughed but the man found out he made a fool of himself and never came back but it is laughable how some people will talk. I often laugh how often I have been dead and buried and turn up some place full of life; there are quite a few that want me to write up things but as they don't want to give me anything I don't write

Well Dear Lillie I hope you won't tire reading this, some is sad and some is quite laughable, but such is life any way we take it; Let me hear from you soon; Hope you will have a nice Easter.

Love and best wishes from Aunt Mary

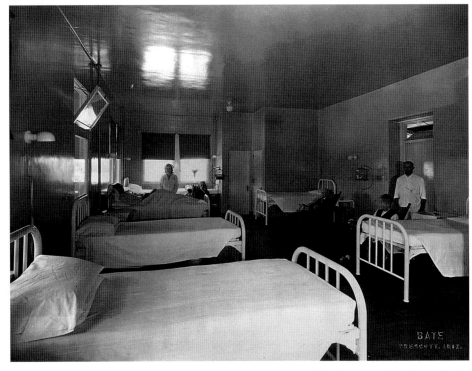

The hospital room at Arizona Pioneer Home. In a room like this one, Big Nose Kate spent her last days as a ward of the state.
(SHARLOT HALL MUSEUM LIBRARY/ARCHIVES, PRESCOTT, ARIZONA)

"I hope you won't tire of reading this, some is sad and some is quite laughable, but such is life any way you take it."
—BIG NOSE KATE

"I often laugh how often I have been dead and buried and turn up some place full of life."
—MARY K. CUMMINGS
(ALIAS "BIG NOSE KATE")

Big Nose Kate's Gravesite (BOYER COLLECTION, SHARLOT HALL MUSEUM LIBRARY/ARCHIVES, PRESCOTT, ARIZONA)

PART THREE

Showtime!

Stacey Keach as "Doc," 1971

DOCTOR WHO?

These actors have portrayed Doc Holliday in movies and on TV.

Movies

Harry Carey, *Law And Order*, 1932

Harvey Clark, *Law for Tombstone*, 1937

Cesar Romero, *Frontier Marshal*, 1939

Walter Houston, *The Outlaw*, 1940

Kent Taylor, *Tombstone, the Town Too Tough to Die*, 1943

Victor Mature, *My Darling Clementine*, 1946

Chubby Johnson, *Law and Order*, 1953

James Griffith, *Masterson of Kansas*, 1954

Kirk Douglas, *Gunfight at the O.K. Corral*, 1957

Arthur Kennedy, *Cheyenne Autumn*, 1964

Jason Robards, *Hour of the Gun*, 1967

Stacey Keach, *Doc*, 1971

William Berger, *Verflucht Dies Amerika*, 1973

Val Kilmer, *Tombstone*, 1993

Dennis Quaid, *Wyatt Earp*, 1994

TV Shows

Douglas Fowley, *The Life and Legend of Wyatt Earp*

Myron Healey, *The Life and Legend of Wyatt Earp*

Dewey Martin, *Dick Powell's Zane Grey Theatre*

Adam West, *Colt .45*

Adam West, *Sugarfoot*

Gerald Mohr, *Maverick*

Peter Breck, *Maverick*

Martin Landau, *Tales of Wells Fargo*

Adam West, *Lawman*

Christopher Dark, *Bonanza*

Jack Kelly, *The High Chaparral*

Dennis Hopper, *Wild Times*

Jeffrey De Munn, *I Married Wyatt Earp*

Sam Gilman, *Star Trek Episode 56, Spectre of the Gun*

LAW AND ORDER, 1932

A mere three years after Wyatt Earp's death (1932), "Law And Order" was the first film to tell the Tombstone story. Harry Carey, Sr. played the Doc Holliday character and Walter Houston was the Wyatt Earp character. Interestingly, Carey knew the real Wyatt, having introduced him to John Ford. Later, Houston would play Doc Holliday in "The Outlaw" (1940), making him the only actor to have played both Earp and Holliday.

A TOAST TO THE CUTTING ROOM FLOOR

A scene cut from the final version of "Law And Order" (1932). This film, with its austere tone and dark vision of the cost of justice was a major influence on Kevin Jarre's script for 1993's "Tombstone." When Walter Houston shouts in fury at the town after Harry Carey, Sr. has been killed, the stage is set for Kurt Russell's rage in "Tombstone" when he roars "I'm coming and Hell's coming with me!"

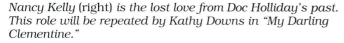

Nancy Kelly (right) is the lost love from Doc Holliday's past. This role will be repeated by Kathy Downs in "My Darling Clementine."

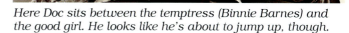

Here Doc sits between the temptress (Binnie Barnes) and the good girl. He looks like he's about to jump up, though.

FRONTIER MARSHAL, 1939

Cesar Romero (above) was the unusual choice to play Doc Holliday in 1939s "Frontier Marshal." Randolph Scott played Wyatt. With blond hair and lean physique, Scott probably holds the strongest resemblance to the real Wyatt of any actor who portrayed Earp. "My Darling Clementine" was actually a remake of "Frontier Marshal" with several incidents repeated in both films. Charles Stevens even plays the same role, Indian Charlie, in both films. Curly Bill was portrayed in this film by veteran character actor Joe Sawyer (he later became Sgt. Biff O'Hara on TV's "Rin Tin Tin").

TOMBSTONE, 1942
Kent Taylor (far left) became the deadly dentist in 1942s "Tombstone." Richard Dix, not shown, was Wyatt. Ike Clanton was played by Victor Jory, while Curly Bill was portrayed by Edgar Buchanan. Despite the fevered memoirs of Ted Ten Eyck—Wallace Beery never played Curly Bill in any film.

GUNFIGHT AT THE O.K. CORRAL, 1957
Kirk Douglas (right) peers through the window of Fly's Photo Gallery after having shot Billy Clanton (Dennis Hopper). Interestingly, Hopper grew up in Dodge City, Kansas where he heard countless tales told about Earp and Holliday. Dennis would later play Doc Holliday in the TV movie "Wild Times" (1980), making him the only actor to play both Billy Clanton and Doc Holliday.

MY DARLING CLEMENTINE, 1946
(l to r: Henry Fonda, Linda Darnell and Victor Mature) Mature was a Twentieth Century Fox contract player Ford really didn't want for the roll. In this film, Holliday is transformed from a Georgia Dentist to a Boston Surgeon who dies at the O.K. Corral. When legend becomes fact, print whatever you damn well please.

LIVER LIPS
Henry Fonda (right) was a laconic Earp and Victor Mature (left) was a beefy Doc Holliday in John Ford's "My Darling Clementine" (1946). Ford kept Mature on edge throughout the shooting by calling him "Liver Lips."

JAILHOUSE DOC
Kirk Douglas (left) as Doc helps Rhonda Fleming get out of jail in 1957s "The Gunfight at the O.K. Corral." Fleming played Laura Denbo, a highly fictionalized version of Lottie Deno, the famous frontier woman gambler who knew Doc at Fort Griffin, Texas.

DEJA VU ALL OVER AGAIN AT THE O.K. CORRAL

In 1957, "The Gunfight at the O.K. Corral" was a top box office draw for Paramount. It's director, John Sturges, was an enormously successful director in the '50s and '60s. Among his other films were "Bad Day at Black Rock," "The Magnificent Seven" and "The Great Escape." Sturges became so fascinated with the story of Doc and Wyatt that ten years after "Gunfight," in 1967, he both produced and directed "Hour of the Gun"—a darker look at the Tombstone story with James Garner and Jason Robards. It is said Lawrence Kasdan is especially fond of Sturges' work. So it is no surprise that in Kasdan's "Wyatt Earp" (1994) the first meeting of Doc and Wyatt mirrors the same moment in "Gunfight at the O.K. Corral." In both films when Wyatt first meets Holliday, Doc is seated alone playing solitaire.

HAVE WHISKEY, WILL DRINK
Jason Robards, as Doc, drinks whiskey and awaits death as James Garner (Wyatt) rides away in a buggy in 1960s "Hour of the Gun." This was Jon Voight's first film. The fair-skinned, stringy blond-haired actor was cast as the swarthy, black-haired Curly Bill Brocious. When legend becomes fact, stand it on its head.

HOUR OF THE GUN, 1967
Wyatt (James Garner) and Doc (Jason Robards) wait for the verdict in Wells Spicer's courtroom. Robards' performance was rich in sarcasm and humor. Garner's Earp was arguably the best performance of his career. Garner is serious, tough and relentless—a far cry from his Maverick and Rockford persona.

DOC'S BAD TRIP

Stacey Keach (far out—right) as a drugged-out Doc playing to an audience which was itself increasingly fried. Doc's habit of drinking a quart of whiskey a day wasn't in line with the times. "Doc" serves as a ready reminder of how we continuously re-vision the past through the lens of the present. Because of this film, Wyatt Earp and Doc Holliday will not ride again on the big screen until 1993.

"Now the only thing a gambler needs, is a suitcase and a trunk, and the only time that he was satisfied was when he was on a drunk."
—"HOUSE OF THE RISING SUN," OLD FOLK SONG

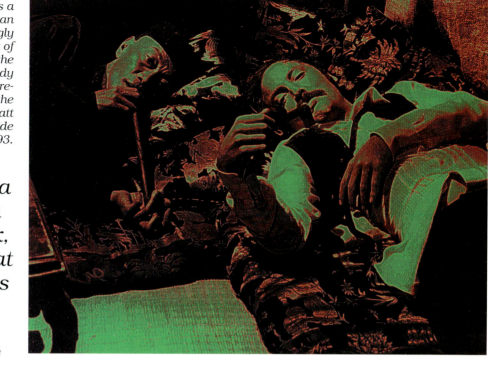

By 1971 the Vietnam War was reshaping Hollywood's attitude towards the Western. Stacey Keach played Holliday and Faye Dunaway (above) was Kate in Frank Perry's "Doc." Laden with symbolism, the Earps became allegorical for the U.S. military, while the Clantons stood in for the Viet Cong. Doc was portrayed as an 'I-don't-give-a-damn, opium-smoking-self-centered-cipher.' Here Hollywood helps kill the Western, ignores history and forgets about drama. Other than that, it's a dynamite film.

Stacey Keach, as "Doc," 1971

YOU'RE NO DAISY
Val Kilmer (left) and Dennis Quaid squared off as Doc Holliday in the two most recent film depictions of the Deadly Dentist. When the smoke cleared, both had scored a bullseye. (PAINTING BY BBB)

DUELING DOCS

Dennis Quaid portrayed Doc Holliday in 1994s "Wyatt Earp" as Bat Masterson described the Deadly Dentist in 1907: "Physically, Doc Holliday was a weakling who could not have whipped a healthy fifteen-year old boy...and the knowledge of this fact was perhaps why he was so ready to resort to a weapon of some kind whenever he got himself into difficulty. He was hot-headed and impetuous and very much given to both drinking and quarreling, and among men who did not fear him, was very much disliked."

Val Kilmer's slant on Doc in 1993s "Tombstone," however, mirrors Wyatt Earp's eulogy to Holliday written in 1896: "He was a dentist, but he preferred to be a gambler. He was a Virginian, but preferred to be a frontiersman and a vagabond. He was a philosopher, but he preferred to be a wag. He was long, lean, and ash blond and the quickest man with a six-shooter I ever knew."

Both performances are dead on.

SPLITTING HAIRS
Both Val Kilmer and Dennis Quaid chose to portray Doc with an imperial (the triangle of whiskers under the lower lip). There is only one alleged photo of Doc Holliday that shows him wearing an imperial (above). Ironically, the photo is not of Doc Holliday.

DOC OUTLIVES "WYATT EARP"

Dennis Quaid's performance in "Wyatt Earp" is too richly realized to be ignored. Warner Brothers and Kevin Costner were reluctant to share stills from their film with us (Warner Brothers' legal department denied us the right to publish any photos from the film). Quaid devastated his body by shedding forty-some pounds to capture the consumptive, cadaver-like Holliday. Bellicose, bilious and as unsavory as a festering canker, this version of Doc Holliday beautifully captures the quality of character which so alienated virtually all who met him. Here we have dissipation personified. Dennis Quaid deserves an Oscar.

"Doc Holliday has become a plum role for any actor. Tragedy and comedy co-mingle in his soul to form a character of infinite complexity."
—JEFF MOREY

Val Kilmer (left) as Doc and Kurt Russell as Wyatt set out on the vengeance trail in 1993s "Tombstone." Kevin Jarre spent well over a year crafting a script that reflected not only history but also the other Earp-Holliday movies. For instance, when the Earps arrive in Tombstone, Virgil (Sam Elliott) mutters the line, "What kind of town is this?" This was a line of Henry Fonda's in "My Darling Clementine." When Doc is leaving Kate (in a scene cut from the film but available on laser disc) he asks, "Have you no kind word for me before I ride away?" This is a wonderful play on the lyrics to Dimitri Tiompkins theme song for "The Gunfight at the O.K. Corral." The lyrics went in part— "Have you no kind word to say before I ride away?"

KURT RUSSELL · VAL KILMER

"One Of The Year's 10 Best!"
—KCOP-TV, Los Angeles

GEORGE P. COSMATOS film

TOMBSTONE

JUSTICE IS COMING!

Three Australian tourists (above) *stop to read the Doc Holliday sidewalk plaque on fashionable Fifth Avenue in Scottsdale, Arizona.* (PHOTO BY BBB)

"Never eat at a cafe named Mom's. Never play cards with a man named Doc..."
—OLD VAQUERO SAYING

DOC'S HOLIDAY?

He was a frontier bum, a disease-ridden drunk and a cold-blooded killer. So why do we love him for it? The answer to that question says more about us than it does about John Henry Holliday.

Against all the tenents of common decency, his name permeates our culture and his visage lurks just beneath the surface as a symbol of...something. What? Could it be Death Denied?

And so today he deserves a national holiday. Call it Holliday's Holiday. On October 26 of every year all U.S. dentists would be encouraged to carry shotguns to work. How about a coin with the slogan "I'll be your huckleberry" with a chiseled image of Doc flipping off the Grim Reaper? Write your congressperson today and insist they act on this piece of important legislation. Sign off with "You're a daisy if you do."

ASPIRING DOCS
Tommy "Doc" and "Barefoot Curly" Bill declare that "this fights commenced; get to fighting or get out!" (PHOTO BY BBB)

Doc Holliday Tavern, Glenwood
Springs, Colorado, 1984 (PHOTO BY BBB)

ICON CITY

*Doc Holliday's of Leadville
(above), is an Old West
Photography studio in Mannie
Hyman's old saloon.
The Doc Holliday liquor
decanter (right), is available
from Early West, College
Station, Texas, $160. (Certainly
the most fitting memorial and
one Doc would love.)*

*"I mixed up with everything that came
along. It was the only way in which I could
forget myself."*

—DOC HOLLIDAY, ONE OF THE WEST'S MOST
UNFORGETTABLE CHARACTERS

*Inside the O.K. Corral grounds some visitors swear they can see and hear the
past. In 1994 over 300,000 tourists from all over the world made the trek to
Tombstone to see "Where they walked, and where they fell."* (PHOTO BY BBB)

GUNFIGHT AT THE OVER & OVER CORRAL

Somewhere, even as you read this, someone is re-enacting the Gunfight at the O.K. Corral. Whether in an organized group or in the back yard, it has become a perpetual re-enactment. Over and over they walk and fall, and rise again. The fight that never ends.

1. **"APPOINTMENT WITH DESTINY— SHOWDOWN AT THE O.K. CORRAL"** 1971 (DAVID L. WOLPER PRODUCTIONS)
2. **WILD BUNCH RE-ENACTMENT,** Tombstone, Arizona, 2:30 p.m., October 26, 1981 (PHOTOS BY BBB)
3. **ARIZONA GUNFIGHTERS,** Rockin' R Ranch, 1989 (BOB CHARNES PHOTOS)
4. **"HOUR OF THE GUN"** 1967 (MIRISCH/KAPPA FILM)
5. **JIM DUNHAM, FOREST PARK ILLINOIS** 1959
6. **RICHARD IGNASKI,** Tombstone, Arizona, October 26, 1981 (PHOTOS BY BBB)
7. **ARIZONA SHOOTISTS,** 10:42:07 a.m. August 5, 1993, Pioneer, Arizona (PHOTOS BY BBB)
8. **THE CALIFORNIA GUNFIGHTERS** from Sacramento, California. October 26, 1881
9. **"TOMBSTONE"** 1993 (HOLLYWOOD PICTURES)
10. **"GUNFIGHT AT THE O.K. CORRAL"** 1957 (PARAMOUNT PICTURES)
11. **"LAW AND ORDER"** 1932 (UNIVERSAL PICTURES)
12. **"STAR TREK—SPECTER OF THE GUN"** TV Episode 56 (PARAMOUNT PICTURES)

1

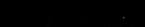

3

9

1

7

1

2

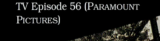

7

1

And now ladies and gentlemen, the way it actually happened... • And now ladies and gentlemen, the way it act

And now ladies and gentlemen, the way it actually happened... • And now ladies and gentlemen, the way it act

1

1

2

1

2

7

2

To Be Continued...

CREDIT WHERE CREDIT IS DUE

This book is dedicated to Theresa Broniarczyk. If Cameron hadn't mowed the lawn, there would be no Billy. If Chris hadn't spotted me the money, there would be no Wyatt. If you hadn't worked around the clock, there would be no Doc. Thank you.

DESIGN AND COMPUTER GRAPHICS

Typography, layout, color, photo enhancement and electronic wizardry by Tri Star Commercial Printing, Chris Sicurella and Brad Ruminer.

WRITTEN BY

Bob Boze Bell and Jeff Morey

ADDITIONAL HISTORICAL RESEARCH

Bob Palmquist, Carl Chafin, Casey Tefertiller, Allen Barra, Jim Dunham

EDITED BY

Marianne Lasby

MODELS

J.D. Holman, Matt "Walker" Obele, Jack Albert, Philip E. Carlin, Jenny Smith, Debra Dodds, Jerry & Von Lee Guerich, John Cochran, Gary Lehmann, Richard, G. Dobberstein, Jeff Morey, Ken Lundskow, Old West Arizona Rangers Historical Society, Wells Twombly, Jim Dunham, Thunderbolt.

SPECIAL THANKS TO

Craig Fouts for the use of his many photos, including the never-before-published picture of Doc and his mother; Michael Wurtz at Sharlot Hall Museum, Prescott, Arizona; Phil Spangenberger; Jan Harrison; Gene Autry Museum; Eddie Brandt's movie stills service; Wells Twombly and John Cochran of Arizona Pioneer Living History Museum; Paul Northrop and Outrider Tours; Bob McCubbin for his steadfast help and access to his magnificent photo collection; Bruce and Alana Coons for the use of their photos; Dave Ritter, for his invaluable technical advice; Tracy Broniarczyk, her fingers tap-tap-tapped away.

DOCTORED & RE-ENACTMENT PHOTOS

(BBB*)

All photos marked as BBB are from the author's collection. All photos marked BBB* are re-enactment photos, and/or doctored. A prime example is the Fly's card on page 81. This photo originated during a re-enactment shoot at Arizona Pioneer Living History Museum using members from the Arizona Rangers. The setting is the Victorian House, or "Vic," as it's called by the crew. The resulting photograph, shot in 35mm color, was then scanned into Photoshop on a Macintosh 8100 Power PC where Chris Sicurella added blood (in color) and aged the photo. The Fly card was extracted from the Ed Schieffelin photo from *Wyatt Earp, page 26.* The two images were then composited, converted to black and white and colorized. Everyone asks why C.S. Fly didn't take any photos after the fight. We think if he had, they would have looked like the card dé visit on page 81.

ABOUT *THE WORLD OF DOC HOLLIDAY* PHOTO *(page 1)*

Original 19th century roulette table backing, displaying various cigarette trading cards. Color cards are lithographs, circa 1880s, photos are circa 1880s -1890s. The playing cards were from a cigarette/tobacco company. The vintage stereo card is of actual prostitutes and the legend at the bottom states "Pay your money, take your choice." Items are shown with vintage gambling chips, a sterling silver and engraved horseshoe-shaped match safe, an 1860s-vintage Sheffield, England-made Manson dirk with etched legend, "Never draw me without reason, nor sheath me without honour." Knife handle is of cutlery type. Suicide Special revolver is a nickel-plated, Red Jacket No.3, 32 caliber, engraved and pearl stocked. Courtesy of Phil Spangenberger collection, photo by Charlie Rathbun.

THE *FINAL,* FINAL JOKE

This is an actual BBB concept sketch that later—much later—Bob finally illustrated after threats that we would use it as is. We all liked it so much though...we decided to use it anyway *(see finished illustration on page 89).*

Printed in Phoenix, Arizona by Tri Star Commercial Printing on 80# Richgloss coated book.